MACMILLAN EXAMS

D1484660

DIRECT TO TOEFL iBT™

Student's Book

Lin Lougheed

MACMILLAN

Macmillan Education
Between Towns Road, Oxford OX4 3PP
A division of Macmillan Publishers Limited
Companies and representatives throughout the world

ISBN 978 0230 40178 5

Text © Lin Lougheed 2011

Design and illustration ©Macmillan Publishers Limited 2011

First published 2011

All rights reserved; no part of this publication may be
reproduced, stored in a retrieval system, transmitted in any
form, or by any means, electronic, mechanical, photocopying,
recording, or otherwise, without the prior written permission
of the publishers.

Design by xen
Cover design by Mark Willey at Designers' Collective
Illustrated by Oxford Designers & Illustrators

The author and publishers would like to thank the following
for permission to reproduce their photographs:

Alamy/Robert Fried p227, Alamy/Glow Asia p268, Alamy/
GoGo Images p190, 281 Alamy/I Love Images p187,
Alamy/Image Source pp34 (t), 39, Alamy/MBI p40, Alamy/
Keith Morris p140, Alamy/Photofusion Picture Library p142,
Alamy/Radius Images p282,
Alamy/Upper Cut Images p188;
Corbis/Fancy p275, Corbis/Flame p34 (b), Corbis/
Moodboard p273, Corbis/Solus p189, Corbis/Spirit p38 (b),
Getty Images p38 (t), Getty Images/Creative p113, Getty
Images/Image Bank p280, Getty Images/Stockbyte p143;
Photolibrary/Blend Images p33 (b), Photolibrary/Robert
Llewellyn p271, 136, 139,
Photolibary/Radius p33 (t), Photolibrary/81a81a p113.

The author would like to thank the many teachers and
students around the world who tested the materials in this
book and whose insights and comments made this book the
perfect TOEFL ibt™ preparation book.

Printed and bound in Thailand

2015   2014   2013   2012   2011
10   9   8   7   6   5   4   3   2   1

DIRECT TO TOEFL iBT™ CONTENTS

Learning English and preparing for the TOEFL iBT™ test are serious commitments of time, energy, and money. You don't want to waste your time, your energy, or your money; you want to use them well. You must make a commitment to yourself to learn English and prepare for the TOEFL iBT™ test.

This is a very serious time in your life. What happens in your future depends on how committed you are to studying and learning. Therefore, you should make a contract with yourself to study English.

Complete this contract with yourself.

MY Direct to TOEFL iBT™ STUDY CONTRACT

I, _____, commit to studying for the TOEFL iBT™.
I will use Direct to TOEFL iBT™, and I will study on my own as well.
I understand that in addition to learning about the TOEFL iBT™, I need to work on improving my English skills in general.

I commit to studying English for _____ hours a week.

I will spend _____ hours a week studying with Direct to TOEFL iBT™.

I will spend _____ hours a week studying English on my own.

I agree to fulfill the terms of this contract.

_____   _____
Signed   Date

Using Direct to TOEFL iBT™

Direct to TOEFL iBT™ combines this study book with Internet-based materials. This book will give you a solid preparation for the TOEFL iBT™ exam. The Internet-based materials at www.directtotoeflibt.com will give you additional practice plus support materials.

Direct to TOEFL iBT™ Student Book includes the following:

- The introduction, which will help you familiarize yourself with the TOEFL iBT™ and begin to improve skills needed on all sections of the test
- Skills and strategies practice sections for each of the four test sections
  - Reading
  - Listening
  - Speaking
  - Writing

  Each section includes a description with sample screens and skills and strategy practice. Each section has a practice test for the particular section.
- A complete practice test

Direct to TOEFL iBT™ website includes the following:

- Three complete practice tests
  - which each contain new passages and questions
  - timed to simulate the actual test experience
- Downloadable answer keys
  - for all practice and test material in the Student Book
  - for all practice and test material online
- Downloadable audio scripts
  - for all audio material in the Student Book
  - for all practice and test material online
- Teacher support materials
- Downloadable audio files for all audio material in the Student Book

Study Plans

Think about how much time you have during the week to prepare for the TOEFL iBT™, as well as how much time you have before your planned test date. Make some decisions ahead of time about how you would like to approach the materials in this Student Book and online.

Here are two possible Study Plans.

Study Plan 1

- Read the Introduction.
- Take the complete practice test in the Student Book to mark your starting point.
- Study the sections where you need more help.
- Take the practice tests after those sections.
- Take a second complete practice test to measure improvement.
- Take the third and the fourth complete practice tests to measure improvement.
- Congratulate yourself on your improved score.

Study Plan 2

- Read the Introduction.
- Take the complete practice test in the Student Book to mark your starting point.
- Study the sections in the order of the test: Reading, Listening, Speaking, Writing.
- Take the practice test after each section.
- Take a second complete practice test to measure improvement.
- Go back and review sections where you want higher scores.
- Retake the section tests.
- Take the third and fourth complete practice tests to measure improvement.
- Congratulate yourself on your improved score.

Each section of the test has its own section in this book. You can start with Reading and study the chapters in the same order as they appear on the test, or you can follow a different order. You can start with the section where you think you need the most help. Once you start a section, you should complete it before going on to another.

At the end of each section, you will find a complete TOEFL iBT™ section practice test. Combined with the complete practice test in the Student Book and the three complete practice tests online at www.directtotoeflibt.com you have four full-length exams that match the format and level of the actual TOEFL iBT™ test. These realistic practice tests and the extensive Student Book and online practice will help you improve your score on the TOEFL iBT™ test.

Extra Activities

There are many ways you can study English on your own. Below are some ideas. Put a checkmark next to the ideas you try, and add your own ideas to the list as well.

Internet-Based Activities

Listening

___ Podcasts on the Internet

___ News websites: CNN, BBC, NBC, ABC, CBS

___ Movies and TV shows in English

___ Academic lectures online

___ Other: _____

Speaking

___ Use Skype to talk to English speakers

___ Other: _____

Writing

___ Write e-mails to website contacts

___ Write a blog about your opinions on any topic

___ Leave comments on blogs

___ Write reviews of books or products on Amazon.com and other websites

___ Other: _____

Reading

___ Read news and magazine articles online

___ Do web research on topics that interest you

___ Follow blogs that interest you

___ Read reviews of books or products on Amazon.com and other websites

___ Other: _____

Other Activities

Listening

___ Listen to English language radio

___ Watch TV news and talk shows in English

___ Watch movies and TV in English

___ Listen to audiobooks in English

___ Listen to people speaking English around you

___ Other: _____

Speaking

___ Describe your daily activities out loud

___ Find a conversation buddy

___ Start an English language book discussion group

___ Join others for lunch or dinner and conversation in English

___ Make phone calls and leave messages in English

___ Other: _____

Writing

___ Write a daily journal

___ Write sentences about things around you

___ Write a letter to an English speaker

___ Write a letter to the editor of an English language newspaper

___ Write descriptions of your family and friends

___ Other: _____

Reading

___ Read newspapers and magazines in English

___ Read books and stories in English

___ Read package labels and instructions in English

___ Other: _____

TOEFL iBT™ Test Skills

Format of the Test

Before you take the TOEFL iBT™ test, you should be comfortable with what to expect in each section of the test. Test day is <u>not</u> the day to see TOEFL iBT™ direction lines or computer screens for the first time. You should be thoroughly familiar with all the things that are the same on each TOEFL iBT™ test.

You must be familiar with

> ➢ what you will see on the computer,

> ➢ how to use the keyboard and toolbar, and

> ➢ what the directions are.

You should not have to think about these when you see them. They should be as familiar as the back of your hand.

The Computer

Before you take the TOEFL iBT™, you need to know how to use a computer. If you already know how to use a mouse or a touchpad, you will be able to move through the sections easily. You will need to move the **cursor** to click on answers and buttons. The cursor is the pointer that shows where you are on the screen.

You will need to type your essays in the Writing section. The faster you can type, the faster you can write and revise.

Keyboard

You must be comfortable using a **QWERTY** keyboard. This is the standard keyboard for English-language computers. The name "QWERTY" comes from the first six letters on the left in the top row of the keyboard.

In the Writing section, you will use the simple commands "cut," "paste," and "undo". These commands are on the part of the test screen where you will write, so there is no need to use actual keyboard commands. These screens and commands are discussed further in the Writing section of the Student Book.

Toolbars

The screen displays of the TOEFL iBT™ are very simple. You should understand the various parts of the displays. The **toolbar** is at the top of each screen. Your movements through a section are controlled by the buttons on these toolbars. The toolbars on the following pages are similar to the ones you will see on the test.

Tip	The toolbars are slightly different in each section, AND how you navigate is different as well.

Toolbar Reading

Test Section	Question Number
Reading	6 of 14

Test Section	This box tells you which section of the test you are in.
Question Number	This box shows which question you are on and how many are left. For example, 6 of 14 tells you there are 14 questions total, and you are on question number 6.
Review	This button takes you to a screen that shows which questions you have answered. From there, you can go back to any Reading question you choose. You can change an answer if you want.
Help	This button takes you to information about the screen functions or question types.
Back	This button, which only appears in Reading, takes you back to previous questions. In Reading, you can go back and change an answer if you want.
Next	This button records your answer and sends you to the next question.
Time	This timer tells you how many minutes are left in the Reading section. You can click on Hide Time if you don't want to see the timer, but it's better to keep track of the time.

Toolbar Listening

Test Section	Question Number
Listening	31 of 34

Test Section	This box tells you which section of the test you are in.
Question Number	This box shows which question you are on and how many are left. For example, 31 of 34 tells you there are 34 questions total, and you are on question number 31.
Help	This button takes you to information about the screen functions or question types.
OK	This button confirms your answer and sends you to the next question. You cannot go back or change answers in Listening after you click OK.
Next	After you choose an answer, click NEXT. You can still change the answer if you want to. You must choose an answer. You cannot click OK if the question is unanswered. A screen will remind you to choose an answer if you click NEXT before you answer.
Time	This timer tells you how many minutes are left in the Listening section. You can click on Hide Time if you don't want to see the timer, but it's better to keep track of the time.
Volume	This button lets you adjust the audio volume.

IMPORTANT: You must click NEXT, then OK to record your answer in Listening. After you click OK, you cannot return to a question.

Toolbar Speaking

Test Section	Question Number
Speaking	2 of 6

Next   Volume   16:29

Test Section	This box tells you which section of the test you are in.
Question Number	This box shows which question you are on and how many are left. For example, 2 of 6 tells you there are 6 questions total, and you are on question number 2.
Volume	This button lets you adjust the audio volume.

IMPORTANT: You have a different amount of time to prepare and speak for different types of questions.

Toolbar Writing

Test Section	Question Number
Writing	1 of 2

Continue   Volume   16:29

Test Section	This box tell you which section of the test you are in.
Question Number	This box shows which question you are on and how many are left. For example, 1 of 2 tells you there are 2 questions total, and you are on question number 1.
Volume	This button lets you adjust the audio volume.
Time	The timer in Writing has two functions.
	1. First, the timer shows how much time you have to read the passage on the screen. When time is up, the screen automatically moves to the audio.
	2. After the audio, the screen moves to the question and the reading passage comes up again. Now the timer tells you how much time you have to write your answer. You can click on Hide Time if you don't want to see the timer while you write, but it's better to keep track of the time.

Directions

The direction lines in this book are similar to the ones on the actual TOEFL iBT™. If you understand the general directions in each section of the test when they appear on the computer screen, you will not have to read them again. You can save time and start previewing the questions, or answering them right away.

Sample directions are included in each section in the Student Book. They include general directions and directions for specific question types.

Taking Notes

Note-taking is an important skill for the TOEFL iBT™. You should practice taking notes on all the sections of the TOEFL iBT™. Here, you will learn note-taking skills for reading and listening. This will in turn help you with note-taking skills for writing and speaking.

> **Tip** You may take notes on all sections of the TOEFL iBT™. You must leave your notes with the test administrator when you finish the test, but they are not graded.

Reading

Establishing Contexts

Understanding the general context of a passage BEFORE you read will help you understand the passage AS you read. Answering these questions will help you establish the context for a passage as well as its content.

- WHAT is the passage about?
- WHERE does it take place?
- WHEN does it take place?
- WHO is important in the passage?
- WHY is the author writing this passage?

Skimming and Scanning

To understand the context, you need to skim and scan. You need to learn to skim and scan in order to find key words and make assumptions about the context.

Skimming is looking over the entire passage quickly. Skimming will give you a *general* idea of what the passage is about. **Scanning** is looking quickly for *specific* information or types of information. Scanning will help you locate answers to questions, and it will also give you a specific idea of what the passage is about.

When you skim, you collect *key words and ideas* that will help you establish the context. As you read, you should be thinking of other words that are associated with these key words. For example, the key word *desert* is often associated with words like *arid*, *dry*, *sandy*, *barren*.

Key words and associated words will help you make assumptions, logical *guesses*, about the context of the passage. You can ask yourself the following questions:

- What do I know about the subject already?
- What will I learn about the subject?
- How is what I know about the subject and what I learn different?

Your own ideas and previous knowledge of the subject will help you understand the passage better. Your assumptions may be wrong, but that does not matter. You read to test your assumptions. If you discover when you read the passage that your assumptions are wrong, it means you comprehend and are analyzing the passage.

Reading is an active process. Your brain must always be working, but you do not have to read every single word to find key words and ideas, or to make assumptions. Skimming and scanning allow you to process information quickly.

Skimming these parts of a passage help you establish the context:
- the title
- graphics
- the first paragraph of the passage
- the first sentences of each paragraph of the passage

Skimming gives you a general idea of the context. You need more information to answer questions about *what, where, when, who,* and *why.* You will need to scan for specific information to understand the passage and answer questions.

You will scan a TOEFL iBT™ passage for specific information:
- other words associated with key words and ideas
- confirmation of assumptions you made
- questions and answer options

The faster you can scan for specific information, the faster you will be able to read and comprehend the passage.

Skimming for key words and ideas, making assumptions, and scanning for specific information will help you focus your reading.

> **Tip**
>
> You won't be able to underline key words in a passage on a computer screen, but you can take notes. Write down key words and assumptions as your notes for a reading passage. Practicing taking notes when you read will help you when you have to listen and take notes.

Model

Look at the following passage. Shading words identify what a reader might skim. The underlined words identify what a reader might scan. These provide clues to the context of the passage. On the right side of the page are assumptions the reader might make.

Formation of Clouds

1 Solutions made of solids in liquids, such as salt in water, are familiar, as are solutions of liquids in liquids, such as vinegar in water, and gases in liquids, such as the oxygen in water that fish breathe. Surprisingly, solutions that at first seem impossible, such as a liquid dissolved in a gas, are also familiar. Liquid water dissolved in air is what fog and clouds are, tiny droplets of water suspended in air.

rain, weather or climate, water cycle

clouds are a type of solution

2 Water has astounding properties that allow it to dissolve in air as well as be a major component of life. The reason is simple although the effects are complex: water molecules are attracted to each other with terrific strength. Water can hold together as drops suspended from a faucet; they can hold together even when the water level is slightly above the lip of a glass; they can hold together as droplets when they are suspended in air. Yet they are light enough to bounce around in air without falling down. Only when enough water molecules congregate in drops and become too heavy do they fall as rain.

water dissolved air becomes clou

3 As water evaporates into the atmosphere, water is suspended in the air. Warmer air can hold more water molecules suspended in it than cooler air. Warmer molecules move faster, zooming around, bumping into each other. Although water molecules suspended in air are attracted to each other, they and the air molecules colliding with them are moving too fast to allow the water molecules to stick together. As air cools, the air and water molecules slow, and when water molecules bump into each other, they stick together and form droplets. When more water droplets bump into each other and stick, they form drops. When drops become large and heavy enough, they cannot remain suspended in the air surrounding them. This is how rain falls and how dew forms. This is why containers of cold drinks are covered in condensed water: The colder air around the drink is unable to keep the water suspended in it, and the glass or can acts as a surface for water droplets to collect as they fall out of the air.

what happens wh water is suspend in air

4 As water evaporates into the atmosphere, it rises. In general, the higher the air in the atmosphere, the colder it is. As water molecules rise, they slow and coalesce, forming droplets. These droplets remain suspended in the rarified air high above us. Since these droplets scatter light, they appear white to us, and we call them "clouds". As the droplets gather in the cloud, the droplets can become bigger and heavier, thus making the clouds appear darker. Eventually the droplets become too large and too heavy to remain suspended and fall down to the surface as rain.

what happens wh water rises in a

When air rises rapidly and <u>water droplets cool</u> high in the atmosphere, they can <u>freeze</u>, and these frozen droplets can <u>remain in suspension</u>. Some of the highest clouds are made of ice crystals in solution in air, a solid dissolved in a gas. These high ice clouds often refract the light reflected off the moon, creating a rainbow halo around the moon. Depending on the size and the shape of the ice crystals, there can be double rainbows around the moon.

The face of the <u>land</u> on earth is <u>shaped</u> to a large extent <u>by</u> this solution of <u>water in air</u>. As water evaporates and rises, it is carried by the prevailing winds, which are from the west in North America. Meeting a mountain range, the air sweeps upward and cools; the suspended water forms droplets, which form into clouds and eventually fall as rain. The air that reaches the eastern slopes is dry. As a result, the western slopes of mountains are rainy and green while the eastern slopes are arid. For example, the western slopes of the Cascade Range are green with vegetation, and Seattle has some of the highest rainfall amounts in the country. The eastern slopes of the Sierra Nevada and Rocky mountains are the Mohave Desert and the arid Great Plains respectively. Such variations in landscapes and climates covering thousands of square miles of the surface of the earth are caused by the attraction of tiny water droplets in solution in the air.

water in clouds can be frozen

effect of rain on the landscape

rain affects climate

Practice 1

Read these titles. Look at the underlined key words. Write down all the associated ideas or words you can think of.

1. <u>Biomimicry</u>: How <u>Humans</u> Have Learned to <u>Imitate</u> <u>Nature</u>

   biology   mimic
   _____

2. Paul <u>Cézanne</u>: The <u>Father</u> of <u>Modern Art</u>

   _____

   _____

3. <u>Pidgin</u> <u>Languages</u> and <u>Creoles</u>

   _____

   _____

Practice 2

Look at these graphics. Write down all the associated ideas or words you can think of.

1.

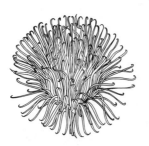 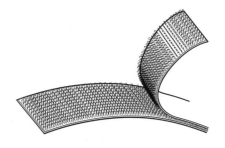

   _____

   _____

2.

   _____

   _____

Practice 3

Read these topic sentences. Look at the underlined key words. Write down all the associated ideas or words you can think of.

1. Billions of years of <u>evolution</u> have resulted in an incredible <u>array</u> of <u>design</u> innovations in <u>nature</u>.

   _____

   _____

2. One well-known brand name, <u>Velcro fasteners</u>, was <u>inspired</u> by a well-known nuisance—<u>burrs</u> getting <u>stuck</u> on a dog's fur.

   _____

   _____

3. Another creative observer of nature, Eiji Nakatsu, drew on his <u>bird-watching</u> hobby to <u>solve</u> an <u>engineering</u> <u>problem</u>.

   _____

   _____

4. Other scientists observed that lotus <u>leaves</u> <u>repel</u> <u>water</u> efficiently.

   _____

   _____

5. <u>Termites</u> inspired <u>architect</u> Mick Pearce.

   _____

   _____

6. When Pearce was asked by his clients to <u>reduce</u> <u>energy</u> needed for <u>temperature</u> control in a climate that fluctuates daily between the 50s and 80s Fahrenheit, he modeled the <u>building</u> on the <u>termite</u> <u>mounds</u> system.

   _____

   _____

7. Another <u>technological</u> <u>advance</u> inspired by analyzing the natural world is <u>tire</u> design.

   _____

   _____

8. Cézanne set himself <u>apart</u> from the <u>Impressionist</u> movement.

   _____

   _____

9. Cézanne <u>painted from nature</u> his entire career: most of his <u>work</u> consists of <u>landscapes</u> and <u>still-lifes</u>.

   _____

   _____

10. Despite <u>little encouragement or recognition</u> from other artists—much less the public—Cézanne <u>painted almost every day</u> of his adult life.

_____

_____

11. Ultimately, why do many <u>artists and art historians</u> call Cézanne—who could be viewed as simply an eccentric post-Impressionist painter who worked alone in southern France far from the cafés and salons—the <u>father of modern art</u>?

_____

_____

12. A pidgin <u>language</u> is a simple language developed to be a <u>means of communication</u> between two or more <u>groups</u> that <u>speak separate languages</u>.

_____

_____

13. <u>Pidgins</u> and <u>creoles</u> are often called <u>contact languages</u> (languages developed from the original contact between two groups) or <u>trade languages</u> (languages developed as a means of conducting trade between speakers of various languages).

_____

_____

14. <u>Hawaiian Creole</u> is a classic <u>example</u> of a <u>pidgin developing into a creole</u>.

_____

_____

15. <u>Gullah</u> is a language still spoken by some <u>descendents of slaves</u> living on sea islands off the coast of Georgia and South Carolina.

_____

_____

16. A <u>French</u>-based <u>creole</u> is spoken in <u>Haiti</u>.

_____

_____

17. <u>Tok Pisin</u>, a <u>creole</u> language that is one of the national languages of <u>Papua New Guinea</u>, actually <u>originated</u> elsewhere, according to scholars.

_____

_____

Practice 4

Look at these questions and answer options. Write down all the associated ideas or words you can think of.

1. According to paragraph 3, Eiji Nakatsu wanted to design a train that would:
   (A) move over water
   (B) make less noise
   (C) travel in tunnels
   (D) look like a bird

   _____

   _____

2. Which of the following can be inferred about the Eastgate office complex?
   (A) Fungus is grown in the basement.
   (B) It was infested with termites at one point.
   (C) It was designed to look like a termite mound.
   (D) A comfortable interior temperature is constantly maintained.

   _____

   _____

3. According to paragraph 2, all of the following are true of Cézanne EXCEPT:
   (A) He was a student of Pissarro's.
   (B) He was part of the Impressionist movement.
   (C) He was fascinated by shapes, forms, and colors.
   (D) He wanted to convey a sense of permanence in his work.

   _____

   _____

4. According to paragraph 5, what is a major reason Cézanne is called the father of modern art?
   (A) He was an important influence on Picasso and Matisse.
   (B) He was the first major post-Impressionist painter.
   (C) He worked alone, so he developed his own style.
   (D) He showed his work in salons and cafés throughout France.

   _____

   _____

5. **Which of the following can be inferred about Hawaiian Creole?**

(A) It has words derived from Japanese and Chinese.

(B) Its grammatical structure is very simple.

(C) It has spread to areas beyond Hawaii.

(D) It is no longer spoken.

6. **Over eight hundred different languages were spoken in Papua New Guinea because**

(A) there were many different ethnic groups

(B) there was a lot of hostility between tribes

(C) people from other islands arrived there in the 1800s

(D) groups were separated by natural features of the land

Adding Details

Understanding how details support ideas is an important reading skill. In Practice 3 above, you made notes on the ideas and key words in topic sentences. Now, look at how details support key words and ideas. Look at these notes for the reading passage, "Formation of Clouds" on page 18. 'Paragraph' is abbreviated as 'para.'.

para. 1   Different kinds of solutions
   A. familiar ones - liquids in liquids, gases in liquids
   B. seems impossible - liquids in gases - clouds, fog

para. 2   Water can dissolve in air
   A. water molecules - strong attraction = water droplets
   B. light enough to stay in air
   C. enough molecules together = fall as rain drops

para. 3   Water evaporates - suspended in air
   A. warm air - fast-moving water molecules - don't stick together
   B. air cools - water molecules slow down, stick together
   C. cool air - rain, dew, condensation

para. 4   Water evaporates - rises
   A. becomes colder - forms drops
   B. drops in air - clouds
   C. becomes heavy - raindrops fall

para. 5   Frozen droplets stay high up in air
   A. ice clouds in air = solution of solid in gas
   B. ice clouds can reflect light of moon

para. 6   Climate is shaped by rain
    A.   wind carries water - clouds form on one side of mountains
    B.   western slopes - green, eastern - dry

Practice 1

Read this passage. You have already seen the key words. Now scan for the supporting details and complete the notes.

Biomimicry: How Humans Have Learned to Imitate Nature

1   Billions of years of evolution have resulted in an incredible array of design innovations in nature. Among other feats, animals, plants, and insects have "learned" to spread seeds, climb vertical surfaces, shed moisture, and moderate the temperatures in their dwellings. While humans have long learned from observing nature, in recent years, designers and engineers have increasingly analyzed and then copied specific designs from the biological world into their innovations and inventions, a process known as "biomimicry".

2   One well-known brand name, Velcro fasteners, was inspired by a well-known nuisance—burrs getting stuck on a dog's fur. In 1941, George de Mestral, a Swiss engineer, became intrigued rather than simply annoyed by burrs and observed them with a microscope. He found that tiny hooks on the burrs were catching on loops in hair or fabric. He used essentially the same design—hooks and loops—and created a new alternative to shoelaces, zippers, buttons and other fastening technology. What had evolved as an efficient seed-dispersal method inspired a fastening method used in clothing and many other applications.

3   Another creative observer of nature, Eiji Nakatsu, drew on his bird-watching hobby to solve an engineering problem. Nakatsu, one of the top engineers of the Shinkansen Bullet Train in Japan, was faced with complaints about the sonic boom made by the 200 mile-per-hour train when it came out of tunnels. He looked for parallels in nature where something moves easily between two different kinds of pressure. He thought of kingfishers, which dive for fish, moving from the air into the water at a high speed, with a minimal amount of splash. When he designed the front of the train to include elements of the design of a kingfisher's head and beak, the train became more efficient—going faster with less energy—as well as much quieter.

4   Other scientists observed that lotus leaves repel water efficiently. Water quickly beads up into drops and rolls off when leaves are tilted even slightly by a breeze or ripple. This action not only removes water; it also removes dirt, which is carried away quickly by the drops. How? The lotus leaves appear smooth but observation with a microscope reveals a rough surface, full of minute cracks that cause round drops to form. A similar design has now been added to the surface of paints and fabrics, allowing them to be much more stain and water-resistant with far fewer chemicals.

5   Termites inspired architect Mick Pearce. He essentially copied the heating and cooling system used in termite mounds to create Eastgate, an office complex in Harare, Zimbabwe, that uses very little heating and no air-conditioning. To grow the fungus that

---

they "farm" for food, termites need to keep their mounds at a constant temperature of 87 degrees F. in a climate that ranges from the thirties to over a hundred degrees. They manage this by creating tunnels in their mounds that draw the air down to mud that they bring up from below. The mud cools the air, and the air is then vented back up through the mound and out a "chimney" at the top. The termites regulate the temperature by plugging holes and digging new ones as needed.

6 When Pearce was asked by his clients to reduce energy needed for temperature control in a climate that fluctuates daily between the 50s and 80s Fahrenheit, he modeled the building on the termite mounds system. Eastgate is essentially two buildings on either side of a shaded atrium that is open to breezes. The cool air of the atrium is pushed by fans up through hollows under the floors and into each office through vents. As the air is heated, it flows upwards and out of the building via a multitude of chimneys. The total system uses under ten percent of the energy of a conventional complex. Savings were also created since no cooling plant needed to be built.

7 Another technological advance inspired by analyzing the natural world is tire design. Tree frogs are able to climb smooth, vertical surfaces. The key to this ability is microscopic hexagonal columns on the surface of their toe pads. Tree frogs secrete a fluid that, when squeezed out between the columns, creates a bond between the toes and whatever the frog is climbing. Engineers have discovered that a similar design for tires enhances a tire's ability to grip wet pavement, reducing sliding and accidents.

para. 1 Evolution – array of designs in nature

A. _____

B. _____

para. 2 Velcro fasteners – inspired by burrs

A. _____

B. _____

C. _____

para. 3 Eiji Nakatsu – Bird-watching solved engineering problem

A. _____

B. _____

C. _____

para. 4 Lotus leaves repel water

A. _____

B. _____

para. 5 Architect inspired by termite mounds

A. _____

B. _____

para. 6 Pearce copied termite mounds system to control building temperature

A. _____

B. _____

para. 7 Tire design inspired by nature

A. _____

B. _____

Practice 2

Read this passage. You have already seen the key words. Now look for the supporting details and complete the notes.

Paul Cézanne—The Father of Modern Art

1   French painter Paul Cézanne was frequently called "the father of modern art". Cézanne was born in 1839 in the city of Aix-en-Provence in the south of France. The son of a wealthy banker, he never had to deal with the poverty that so many of the Impressionist painters before him experienced. He spent most of his life in Aix-en-Provence, with infrequent visits to Paris, the center of the art world of his day.

2   Cézanne set himself apart from the Impressionist movement. His work was never accepted in the salons, and he rarely exhibited with the Impressionists. While he was mentored in Impressionist painting techniques by Pissarro, and he appreciated the work of Manet and Courbet, Cézanne felt that Impressionist painting often lacked structure and focused too much on the impermanence of life. He said, "I wish to make of Impressionism something solid and durable, like the art of the museums." While many of the Impressionists focused on the ephemeral nature of light in different kinds of weather, times of day, and seasons, and often tried to capture the unique qualities of individuals in specific locations and events, Cézanne focused on color, planes, forms, and composition. He was more interested in a sense of permanence and timelessness than in the fleeting nature of the moment. He was more interested in capturing the essence of shapes and forms than in capturing story or personality. Cézanne was fascinated with basic geometric forms such as cones and spheres.

3   Cézanne painted from nature his entire career: most of his work consists of landscapes and still-lifes. His landscapes rarely include people or animals and give few hints about a particular moment. One does not associate a particular time of day, season, or kind of weather with them. A favorite landscape subject is Mont Sainte-Victoire, a mountain that he could see from the home of his sister and brother-in-law. Cézanne painted over 200 still-lifes and famously said that he would "conquer Paris with an apple". Most of the still-lifes are formally arranged groupings of apples, oranges, pears, and cloth. When Cézanne did paint people, their figures and faces served more as elements of composition than as clues to personality and life stories. In his famous painting often called "Large Bathers", Cézanne arranged nudes and tree trunks into a pyramid-shaped composition. There is little detail in the faces or leaves. The painting celebrates the beauty of diagonal and curving lines and planes of color much more than the beauty of nature and the human form.

---

4 Despite little encouragement or recognition from other artists—much less the public—Cézanne painted almost every day of his adult life. He had a vision of a new approach to painting and continued his experiments with observing how colors changed in the natural world and with the effects of placing one color next to another. While Impressionists had worked often with small areas or even tiny dots of color, Cézanne tended to juxtapose different planes of color. His work became more and more abstract in his later years. Only when he was well into his fifties, did he receive recognition when art dealer Ambroise Vollard organized an exhibition of Cézanne's work in Paris in 1895. Two years later Vollard bought every painting in Cézanne's studio. Word spread and young artists began to make pilgrimages to Aix to seek his advice and watch him work.

5 Ultimately, why do many artists and art historians call Cézanne—who could be viewed as simply an eccentric post-Impressionist painter who worked alone in southern France far from the cafés and salons—the "father of modern art"? There are many reasons, but a key reason is that both Pablo Picasso and Henri Matisse, who differed widely from each other but played pivotal roles in the further development of modern art, traced their work back to Cézanne. Picasso further developed Cézanne's emphasis on planes in his cubist phase, and Matisse loved Cézanne's use of color.

para. 1 Paul Cézanne – French painter – father of modern art

A. _____

B. _____

para. 2 Not part of Impressionist movement

A. _____

B. _____

C. _____

para. 3 Painted from nature

A. _____

B. _____

C. _____

para. 4 Painted every day, little encouragement

A. _____

B. _____

para. 5 Why father of modern art?

A. _____

B. _____

Practice 3

Read this passage. You have already seen the key words. Now look for the supporting details and complete the notes.

Pidgin Languages and Creoles

1 A pidgin language is a simple language developed to be a means of communication between two or more groups that speak separate languages. While pidgins may contain words from a variety of languages, one language is dominant—the superstrate language— and the other languages—the substrate languages—contribute fewer words and structure. Often a pidgin starts out with mainly nouns, verbs, and adjectives. Sometimes a pidgin develops a consistent grammar and a more extensive vocabulary and becomes the primary language of a group of people. Then it is called a "creole". Not all pidgins develop into creoles.

2 Pidgins and creoles are often called "contact languages" (languages developed from the original contact between two groups) or "trade languages" (languages developed as a means of conducting trade between speakers of various languages). In fact, the word *pidgin* is thought to be derived from the Cantonese pronunciation of *business*, which became the name for the language that the British used in conducting trade in China in the eighteenth century. The majority of pidgins and creoles developed in situations where colonization or slavery brought speakers of differing languages together into situations where they needed to communicate. In the majority of cases, the superstrate language is French or English. Many pidgins and creoles developed in situations where workers with different native languages were brought together by European or North Americans.

3 Hawaiian Creole is a classic example of a pidgin developing into a creole. When missionaries and businessmen from the United States first came into contact with native Hawaiians, there was no commonly understood language. A simple pidgin developed, based on English, but also including native Hawaiian words and semantic structures. As workers from Japan, the Philippines, China, and other countries were brought to Hawaii to work on the plantations, the pidgin language became enriched with words from many languages, and, as it became the primary language of second and third generation speakers, it developed the complexities of what linguists refer to as a creole. Confusingly, while most linguists call the language Hawaiian Creole, most Hawaiians refer to it as "Hawaiian Pidgin" or simply "Pidgin".

4 Gullah is a language still spoken by some descendents of slaves living on sea islands off the coast of Georgia and South Carolina. Gullah is a remnant of a creole that developed in western Africa during the slave trade in the eighteenth century. Most slave traders spoke English. In order to communicate with the Africans they traded with, they spoke a simplified version of English that also contained elements of various African languages. Gullah also became the lingua franca, common language, in the region among speakers of African languages that included Mende, Fula, and Vai. Many of the slaves brought to the Americas already spoke the West African Creole, and many scholars believe this creole became the basis for communications between slaves. Gullah is primarily made up of English words, but the pronunciation and much of the structure of the grammar is heavily influenced by African languages and a sizeable fraction of the vocabulary comes from different African languages. Many linguists have noted the similarities between Gullah and other English-African creoles spoken in the Caribbean.

5 A French-based creole is spoken in Haiti. The French colonized Haiti and developed slave plantations beginning in the 1700s. As slaves speaking different African languages communicated with each other and the French-speaking masters, a French-based pidgin gradually developed into a unique language that maintained much of the vocabulary of French, but also includes vocabulary and semantic structures of various African languages. Today Kreyòl, Haitian Creole, is the national language of Haiti.

6 Tok Pisin, a creole language that is one of the national languages of Papua New Guinea, actually originated elsewhere, according to scholars. New Guinean workers were recruited to work on sugar plantations in Australia, Samoa, Fiji, and other Pacific islands during the 1800s. Varieties of English-based pidgins developed on the plantations and then were brought back to New Guinea by returning workers. The different clans and tribe of Papua New Guinea were separated by thick jungle and deep ravines and so lived in relative isolation from each other. Because of this situation, over 800 different languages were spoken there. Tok Pisin increasingly became a means of communicating between these language groups as modernity brought more and more contact between them. Tok Pisin developed into a complex language that is spoken as a first language by over twenty thousand people and as a second language by over 40 percent of the population.

para. 1 Pidgin – communication between language groups

A. _____

B. _____

para. 2 Pidgins and creoles – contact languages, trade languages

A. _____

B. _____

para. 3 Hawaiian Creole – example of pidgin developed into creole

A. _____

B. _____

C. _____

para. 4 Gullah – descendents of slaves

A. _____

B. _____

C. _____

para. 5 Haiti – French-based creole

A. _____

B. _____

para. 6 Tok Pisin – a national language of Papua New Guinea, but originated elsewhere

A. _____

B. _____

Listening

Establishing Contexts

Establishing a context while listening can sometimes be difficult. It is like walking down a dark path. You may think you know where you are going, but then you suddenly have to take a turn in another direction. You have to be alert when you listen. Taking notes will help you pay attention.

There are some clues that will help you establish a context for listening:

- graphics (photo)
- first sentences
- questions and answer options

The TOEFL iBT™ provides a photo of the speaker(s) and the setting. You will know if one or more people are talking and if the setting is in a classroom or somewhere else. You can then make an assumption about the purpose. In some cases, your assumption may be wrong. You must listen carefully to test your assumption.

Look at the above photo. We can assume the following:

Speaker(s):	Professor
Setting:	Classroom
Purpose:	Lecture

When you establish a context in reading, you scan for key words. When you read, you first scan for key words and make assumptions about the words and ideas. You do the same thing when you listen, but it is a bit more difficult. When you read, your eye can race ahead. When you listen, your ear depends on the speed of the speaker.

The first couple of sentences in a lecture or conversation are very important. They will establish the topic or context for the listening passage. You can begin to collect key words when you hear these first two or three sentences.

Read these opening sentences and look at the notes (key words) that you might take.

> As you move up a mountain, the conditions change, thus you will find different ecosystems at different altitudes. We're going to take a brief look today at the characteristics of the alpine biome or ecosystem.

Notes:

mountain, ecosystems, characteristics of alpine biome

In the Reading section, you scanned the questions and answers to help establish a context. You can do the same in the Listening section before you hear the lecture or conversation.

Look at these example questions. You can begin to establish a context and make assumptions by looking at what key words the questions and answer choices have in common.

1. What is this lecture mainly about?

   (A) How ecosystems change with altitude

   (B) Conditions of a particular ecosystem

   (C) The life cycle of alpine plants

   (D) Plants that produce seeds

2. How do annual plants survive the cold winter?

   (A) They get warmth from rocks.

   (B) They bury themselves in the soil.

   (C) They are protected by the snow cover.

   (D) They produce seeds which grow the next spring.

Practice 1

Look at the photos and make assumptions about the contexts.

1.

Speaker(s): _____

Setting: _____

Purpose: _____

2.

Speaker(s): _____

Setting: _____

Purpose: _____

3.

Speaker(s): _____

Setting: _____

Purpose: _____

4.

Speaker(s): _____

Setting: _____

Purpose: _____

DIRECT TO TOEFL iBT™

Practice 2

Listen to the opening sentences that go with the photos in Practice 1. What information can you add to your notes?

1. _____

2. _____

3. _____

4. _____

Practice 3

Read these questions and underline the key words. The first one is done for you.

1. **What is this lecture mainly about?**

   (A) An American <u>author</u>
   (B) An American novel
   (C) An American whaling ship
   (D) An American sea captain

2. **What were Melville's first two novels based on?**

   (A) His job as a whaler
   (B) His work on his farm
   (C) His life as a cabin boy
   (D) His experiences in Polynesia

3. **Why is the student talking to the librarian?**

   (A) He wants to borrow some books from the library.
   (B) He wants to apply for a library card.
   (C) He wants to subscribe to a magazine.
   (D) He wants to locate the restricted books.

4. **Where are the restricted books kept?**

   (A) First floor
   (B) Second floor
   (C) Third floor
   (D) Fourth floor

5. **What will the student do next?**

   (A) Go to class

   (B) Read a magazine

   (C) Check out some magazines

   (D) Get a new library card

6. **What is this lecture mainly about?**

   (A) The history of New York City

   (B) The building of the Brooklyn Bridge

   (C) The achievements of the Roebling family

   (D) The development of bridge construction

7. **Why does the lecturer mention skyscrapers?**

   (A) To describe the appearance of New York City

   (B) To explain how impressive the Brooklyn Bridge looked

   (C) To compare building construction with bridge construction

   (D) To give an example of famous New York City landmarks

8. **Why didn't John Roebling supervise the entire construction of the Brooklyn Bridge?**

   (A) He was lame due to an injured foot.

   (B) He suffered from the bends.

   (C) He lost his ability to talk.

   (D) He died of tetanus.

9. **Why is the student talking to the professor?**

   (A) She needs help choosing a research topic.

   (B) She wants more time to complete her assignment.

   (C) She wants to know when the research project is due.

   (D) She needs help finding books and journals.

10. **When is the research project due?**

    (A) In two weeks

    (B) In three weeks

    (C) Next month

    (D) At the end of the semester

11. **What does the professor give the student?**

    (A) A copy of a journal article

    (B) A list of topics

    (C) A project outline

    (D) A journal subscription

Adding Details

Once you have established the context, you will need to listen carefully for details. These details are often in the same sentence or very close to the key word.

Read this lecture. Look at the notes (key ideas) that you might make and look at the details that are given.

Lecture:

As you move up a mountain, the conditions change, thus you'll find different ecosystems at different altitudes. We're going to take a brief look today at the characteristics of the alpine biome or ecosystem. What do we mean when we talk about the "alpine zone"? It's the area that you find at a high altitude, above the tree line and below the snow line, that is, the area of permanent snow cover. You'll find vegetation in the alpine zone, but it's all low-growing plants, not trees. The alpine zone usually begins at an altitude of about 10,000 feet. Temperatures are around 10 degrees centigrade in the summer and below freezing in the winter.

Plants have developed certain adaptations to the conditions of the alpine zone. For example, the growing season is short, four months at the most, and not very warm. This is too short a time for trees to produce enough food to support a woody trunk as well as branches and leaves, so you won't find any trees. On the other hand, you will find a number of annual plants, that is, fast-growing plants with short life cycles. In one summer, an annual plant grows, flowers, and produces seeds. These plants survive the winter in the form of their seeds, which remain in the soil and sprout the following spring.

Conditions in the alpine zone are often quite windy and cold. You'll find many plants that grow low to the ground, where they're protected from the wind and cold. For example, low-growing shrubs are characteristic of the alpine zone. They often cling to rocks where they can take advantage of the heat absorbed by the rocks. The wind and cold also result in poor soil conditions. The wind blows soil away, and because of the cold, dead plants are slow to decompose.

Notes:

idea 1 Alpine zone – what is it?
A.   between tree line and snow line
B.   vegetation (not trees)
C.   10 degrees to below freezing

idea 2 Short growing season
A.   too short for trees
B.   good for annual plants-grow fast

idea 3 Windy and cold conditions
A.   plants – low to the ground
B.   shrubs get warmth from rocks
C.   poor soil – wind and slow decomposition

Practice 1

Listen to this lecture. Write down the key ideas and at least two details for each. The number of key ideas is given.

idea 1:_____

A._____

B._____

idea 2:_____

A._____

B._____

idea 3:_____

A._____

B._____

Practice 2

Listen to this conversation. Write down the key ideas and at least two details for each. The number of key ideas is given.

idea 1:_____

A._____

B._____

idea 2:_____

A._____

B._____

idea 3:_____

A._____

B._____

Practice 3

Listen to this lecture. Write down the key ideas and at least two details for each. The number of key ideas is given.

idea 1:_____

A._____

B._____

idea 2:_____

A._____

B._____

idea 3:_____

A._____

B._____

Practice 4

Listen to this conversation. Write down the key ideas and at least two details for each. The number of key ideas is given.

idea 1:_____

A._____

B._____

idea 2:_____

A._____

B._____

idea 3:_____

A._____

B._____

Pace

Timing

There is a set amount of time for each section of the TOEFL iBT™ exam. Each section of the Student Book includes a detailed chart showing the number of questions and amounts of time.

Reading	60–100 minutes
Listening	60–90 minutes
Speaking	20 minutes
Writing	50 minutes

Be sure to leave enough time to answer every question. You don't want to hurry through questions to finish. If you don't know the answer to a particular question, try to eliminate the options you are sure are wrong. Then make a guess with the remaining options.

> **Tip** Remember that the toolbar for Reading, Listening, and Writing includes a timer. The timer tells you how much time you have left.

Many things will affect your speed on the TOEFL iBT™ test.

➤ Your proficiency in English

➤ Your facility with computers and typing

➤ Your understanding of the test format

➤ Your understanding of the directions

➤ Your familiarity with the question types and tasks

This book and the activities on the Direct to TOEFL iBT™ website will help you improve your timing on all sections of the TOEFL iBT™.

Reading Speed

You should practice reading quickly, but also carefully and with comprehension. Before you start to read, you will skim and scan to look for key words and made assumptions. Now you must practice reading faster.

Here are some tips for increasing your reading speed.

Read more than one word at a time. Train your eye to take in large groups of words.

➤ Words that surround key words.
   . . . <u>solutions</u> that at first seem impossible

➤ Words that are in a clause.
   As water evaporates into the atmosphere . . .

➤ Words that surround the subject.
   Liquid <u>water</u> dissolved in air . . .

➤ Words that surround the verb.
   When air <u>rises</u> rapidly . . .

> **Tip** | Skim the reading passage and scroll to the end. Then read the questions carefully and scan for the answers.

This exercise will help you improve your reading speed for the Reading section as well as the questions in the Listening section. You will need a watch with a second hand or the stopwatch on your Smartphone for this exercise.

Practice 1

A. First, read each question. Write down how long it took you to read the question. Then, read each paragraph. Write down how many seconds it took you to read the paragraph.

B. Do this two more times. Is your speed and comprehension improving?

Passage 1

Biomimicry: How Humans Have Learned to Imitate Nature

One well-known brand name, Velcro fasteners, was inspired by a well-known nuisance—burrs getting stuck on a dog's fur. In 1941, George de Mestral, a Swiss engineer, became intrigued rather than simply annoyed by burrs and observed them with a microscope. He found that tiny hooks on the burrs, were catching on loops in hair or fabric. He used essentially the same design—hooks and loops—and created a new alternative to shoelaces, zippers, buttons, and other fastening technology. What had evolved as an efficient seed-dispersal method inspired a fastening method used in clothing and many other applications.

---

1. According to the paragraph, all of the following are true about Velcro EXCEPT:
    (A) Its design is based on hooks and loops.
    (B) It is used to fasten different items of clothing.
    (C) It is used as an efficient way to disperse seeds.
    (D) It was inspired by burrs becoming attached to fur.

Time: _____ _____   Time: _____ _____   Time: _____ _____

Another creative observer of nature, Eiji Nakatsu, drew on his bird-watching hobby to solve an engineering problem. Nakatsu, one of the top engineers of the Shinkansen Bullet Train in Japan, was faced with complaints about the sonic boom made by the 200-mile-per-hour train when it came out of tunnels. He looked for parallels in nature where something moves easily between two different kinds of pressure. He thought of kingfishers, which dive for fish, moving from the air into the water at a high speed, with a minimal amount of splash. When he designed the front of the train to include elements of the design of a kingfisher's head and beak, the train became more efficient—going faster with less energy—as well as much quieter.

---

2. According to the paragraph, Eiji Nakatsu wanted to design a train that would
   (A) move over water
   (B) make less noise
   (C) travel in tunnels
   (D) look like a bird

Time: _____ _____   Time: _____ _____   Time: _____ _____

Other scientists observed that lotus leaves repel water efficiently. Water quickly beads up into drops and rolls off when leaves are tilted even slightly by a breeze or ripple. This action not only removes water, it also removes dirt, which is carried away quickly by the drops. How? The lotus leaves appear smooth, but observation with a microscope reveals a rough surface, full of minute cracks that cause round drops to form. A similar design has now been added to the surface of paints and fabrics, allowing them to be much more stain and water resistant with far fewer chemicals.

3. According to the paragraph, which of the following is a feature of lotus leaves that inspired a way to make fabric resist stains?
   (A) The chemical composition
   (B) The ability to roll up when wet
   (C) The rough surface of the leaves
   (D) The manner of tilting in the breeze

Time: _____ _____   Time: _____ _____   Time: _____ _____

Termites inspired architect Mick Pearce. He essentially copied the heating and cooling system used in termite mounds to create Eastgate, an office complex in Harare, Zimbabwe, that uses very little heating and no air-conditioning. To grow the fungus that they "farm" for food, termites need to keep their mounds at a constant temperature of 87 degrees F. in a climate that ranges from the 30s to over a hundred degrees. They manage this by creating tunnels in their mounds that draw the air down to mud that they bring up from below. The mud cools the air, and the air is then vented back up through the mound and out a "chimney" at the top. The termites regulate the temperature by plugging holes and digging new ones as needed.

4. According to the paragraph, which of the following can be inferred about the Eastgate office complex?
   (A) Fungus is grown in the basement.
   (B) It was infested with termites at one point.
   (C) It was designed to look like a termite mound.
   (D) A comfortable interior temperature is constantly maintained.

Time: _____ _____   Time: _____ _____   Time: _____ _____

Practice 2

Read each question. Then scan each paragraph for the answer. Write down how long it took you to answer each question.

> **Passage 2**
>
> ### Paul Cézanne—The Father of Modern Art
>
> Cézanne set himself apart from the Impressionist movement. His work was never accepted in the salons, and he rarely exhibited with the Impressionists. While he was mentored in Impressionist painting techniques by Pissarro, and he appreciated the work of Manet and Courbet, Cézanne felt that Impressionist painting often lacked structure and focused too much on the impermanence of life. He said, "I wish to make of Impressionism something solid and durable, like the art of the museums." While many of the Impressionists focused on the ephemeral nature of light in different kinds of weather, times of day, and seasons and often tried to capture the unique qualities of individuals in specific locations and events, Cézanne focused on color, planes, forms, and composition. He was more interested in a sense of permanence and timelessness than in the fleeting nature of the moment. He was more interested in capturing the essence of shapes and forms than in capturing story or personality. Cézanne was fascinated with basic geometric forms such as cones and spheres.

1. **According to paragraph 2, all of the following are true of Cézanne EXCEPT:**
   (A) He was a student of Pissarro's.
   (B) He was part of the Impressionist movement.
   (C) He was fascinated by shapes, forms, and colors.
   (D) He wanted to convey a sense of permanence in his work.

Time: _____   Time: _____   Time: _____

Cézanne painted from nature his entire career: most of his work consists of landscapes and still-lifes. His landscapes rarely include people or animals and give few hints about a particular moment. One does not associate a particular time of day, season, or kind of weather with them. A favorite landscape subject is Mont Sainte-Victoire, a mountain that he could see from the home of his sister and brother-in-law. Cézanne painted over 200 still-lifes and famously said that he would "conquer Paris with an apple." Most of the still-lifes are formally arranged groupings of apples, oranges, pears, and cloth. When Cézanne did paint people, their figures and faces served more as elements of composition than as clues to personality and life stories. In his famous painting often called "Large Bathers", Cézanne arranged nudes and tree trunks into a pyramid-shaped composition. There is little detail in the faces or leaves. The painting celebrates the beauty of diagonal and curving lines and planes of color much more than the beauty of nature and the human form.

2. **Why does the author discuss the painting "Large Bathers" in the paragraph?**
   (A) To show that Cézanne could paint people as well as landscapes
   (B) To illustrate Cézanne's focus on form and composition
   (C) To give an example of a famous work by Cézanne
   (D) To explain Cézanne's interest in painting nature

Time: _____   Time: _____   Time: _____

Despite little encouragement or recognition from other artists—much less the public—Cézanne painted almost every day of his adult life. He had a vision of a new approach to painting and continued his experiments with observing how colors changed in the natural world and with the effects of placing one color next to another. While Impressionists had worked often with small areas or even tiny dots of color, Cézanne tended to juxtapose different planes of color. His work became more and more abstract in his later years. Only when he was well into his fifties, did he receive recognition when art dealer Ambroise Vollard organized an exhibition of Cézanne's work in Paris in 1895. Two years later Vollard bought every painting in Cézanne's studio. Word spread and young artists began to make pilgrimages to Aix to seek his advice and watch him work.

3. **According to the paragraph, when did Cézanne start to gain recognition for his work?**
   (A) When he was still a young boy
   (B) In his early adulthood
   (C) When he was close to 60
   (D) After his death

Time: _____   Time: _____   Time: _____

Ultimately, why do many artists and art historians call Cézanne—who could be viewed as simply an eccentric post-Impressionist painter who worked alone in southern France far from the cafés and salons—the "father of modern art"? There are many reasons, but a key reason is that both Pablo Picasso and Henri Matisse, who differed widely from each other but played pivotal roles in the further development of modern art, traced their work back to Cézanne. Picasso further developed Cézanne's emphasis on planes in his cubist phase, and Matisse loved Cézanne's use of color.

4. **According to paragraph 5, what is a major reason why Cézanne is called the father of modern art?**
   (A) He was an important influence on Picasso and Matisse.
   (B) He was the first major post-Impressionist painter.
   (C) He worked alone, so he developed his own style.
   (D) He showed his work in salons and cafés throughout France.

Time: _____   Time: _____   Time: _____

Passage 3

Pidgin Languages and Creoles

Pidgins and creoles are often called "contact languages" (languages developed from the original contact between two groups) or "trade languages" (languages developed as a means of conducting trade between speakers of various languages). In fact, the word *pidgin* is thought to be derived from the Cantonese pronunciation of *business*, which became the name for the language that the British used in conducting trade in China in the eighteenth century. The majority of pidgins and creoles developed in situations where colonization or slavery brought speakers of differing languages together into situations where they needed to communicate. In the majority of cases, the superstrate language is French or English. Many pidgins and creoles developed in situations where workers with different native languages were brought together by European or North Americans.

5. **What can be inferred from the paragraph about pidgins?**
   (A) They are common in Europe and North America.
   (B) Most of them are based on English or French.
   (C) Most eighteenth-century traders spoke them.
   (D) They originally came from China.

Time: _____   Time: _____   Time: _____

Hawaiian Creole is a classic example of a pidgin developing into a creole. When missionaries and businessmen from the United States first came into contact with native Hawaiians, there was no commonly understood language. A simple pidgin developed, based on English, but also including native Hawaiian words and semantic structures. As workers from Japan, the Philippines, China, and other countries were brought to Hawaii to work on the plantations, the pidgin language became enriched with words from many languages and, as it became the primary language of second and third generation speakers, it developed the complexities of what linguists refer to as a "creole". Confusingly, while most linguists call the language Hawaiian Creole, most Hawaiians refer to it as "Hawaiian Pidgin" or simply "Pidgin".

6. Which of the following can be inferred about Hawaiian Creole?
   (A) It has words derived from Japanese and Chinese.
   (B) Its grammatical structure is very simple.
   (C) It has spread to areas beyond Hawaii.
   (D) It is no longer spoken.

Time: _____   Time: _____   Time: _____

Gullah is a language still spoken by some descendents of slaves living on sea islands off the coast of Georgia and South Carolina. Gullah is a remnant of a creole that developed in western Africa during the slave trade in the eighteenth century. Most slave traders spoke English. In order to communicate with the Africans they traded with, they spoke a simplified version of English that also contained elements of various African languages. Gullah also became the lingua franca, common language, in the region among speakers of African languages that included Mende, Fula, and Vai. Many of the slaves brought to the Americas already spoke the West African Creole, and many scholars believe this creole became the basis for communications between slaves. Gullah is primarily made up of English words, but the pronunciation and much of the structure of the grammar is heavily influenced by African languages and a sizeable fraction of the vocabulary comes from different African languages. Many linguists have noted the similarities between Gullah and other English-African creoles spoken in the Caribbean.

7. According to the paragraph, all of the following are true of Gullah EXCEPT:
   (A) It developed out of the slave trade.
   (B) It originated in the Caribbean Islands.
   (C) It has many words derived from African languages.
   (D) It continues to be spoken in the United States today.

Time: _____   Time: _____   Time: _____

Tok Pisin, a creole language that is one of the national languages of Papua New Guinea, actually originated elsewhere, according to scholars. New Guinean workers were recruited to work on sugar plantations in Australia, Samoa, Fiji, and other Pacific islands during the 1800s. Varieties of English-based pidgins developed on the plantations and then were brought back to New Guinea by returning workers. The different clans and tribes of Papua New Guinea were separated by thick jungle and deep ravines, and so lived in relative isolation from each other. Because of this situation, over 800 different languages were spoken there. Tok Pisin increasingly became a means of communicating between these language groups as modernity brought more and more contact between them. Tok Pisin developed into a complex language that is spoken as a first language by over twenty thousand people, and as a second language by over 40 percent of the population.

8. Over 800 different languages were spoken in Papua New Guinea because

  (A) there were many different ethnic groups
  (B) there was a lot of hostility between tribes
  (C) people from other islands arrived there in the 1800s
  (D) groups were separated by natural features of the land

Time: _____   Time: _____   Time: _____

Strategies

General

- Understand the directions and question types before you take the test. Using the "Help" button will slow you down.
- Keep your mind on one question at a time. Don't think back at what you should have answered on an earlier question.
- Keep moving forward. Budget your time. Don't spend too much time on one question.
- Check the clock on the toolbar from time to time and adjust your pace as necessary.

Reading

- Scan the title and passage for key words before reading.
- All the information you need to answer the questions is contained in the passage. You do not need any special background knowledge. If you feel unsure about something, move on.
- You can click on "Back" or "Review" to see your previous answers. However, unless you are sure you want to change something, moving ahead is a better use of your time.

Listening

- Some of the lectures or conversations may have a question about the attitude of the speaker. Pay attention to the tone of voice and overall tone of words that can give you clues about a speaker's attitude.
- Take concise notes and refer to them when answering the questions. Use your own form of shorthand for note-taking.
- Remember that in the Listening section you cannot go back to change an answer once you have clicked "OK".

Speaking

- Speak clearly and at a regular pace so that you can be understood.
- Make sure you answer the question. For some questions you are asked to give your opinion and for others you are asked to summarize and/or analyze information.

Writing

- For the Integrated Writing task, take concise notes while listening and reading and refer to them when planning your essay.
- For both tasks, spend a few minutes outlining your ideas before writing.
- Leave a few minutes at the end for revision and editing.

READING

Facts About Reading

Skills

Basic Comprehension

Reading to Learn

Skills Practice

Reading Practice Test

The Reading section of the TOEFL iBT™ includes three to five passages with 12–14 questions about each passage. All of the passages are on academic topics. You do not need to have any special background knowledge for the Reading section; all the information you need to answer the questions is in the passage itself.

The chart on page 52 shows you what types of questions are included. Pages 53–55 show you examples of what the screens look like for Reading.

Most questions in Reading are multiple-choice with four answer choices and one correct answer. A second question type requires you to insert a sentence at the correct spot in a paragraph. A final question type has more than four answer choices in a chart. Chart-type questions are worth more than one point. You can get partial credit on the chart-type questions.

The entire Reading section takes 60–100 minutes. As in all the sections, you may take notes. Most importantly, you can go back to previous questions and passages in the Reading section only.

Facts About Reading

Content	3–5 passages from academic course books
Length	Approximately 700 words per passage
Questions	12–14 questions per passage = 36–70 questions total
Time	60–100* minutes
Score	0–30
Points	Multiple-choice and insertion questions are 1 point.
	Summary chart questions are up to 2 points.
	Completion chart questions are up to 3 or 4 points.
Type of passages	Explanation
	Point of view
	Historical
Organization	Classification
	Comparison and Contrast
	Cause and Effect
	Problem and Solution
Question formats	Multiple-choice with single answer
	Multiple-choice to insert in text
	Chart/table completion or summary
Question types	Factual information/passage/(3–6 questions)
	Vocabulary (3–5/passage)
	Negative (0–2/passage)
	Inference (0–2/passage)
	Purpose (0–2/passage)
	Reference (0–2/passage)
	Simplification (0–1/passage)
	Text insertion (0–1/passage)
	Summary (0–1/passage)
	Completion (0–1/passage)
Measures ability to	Understand university-level passages
	Skim and scan for major points or facts
	Read fluently and quickly
	Identify main idea and supporting details
	Make inferences
	Recognize organization of passage
	Understand purpose of passage

* Some passages may be experimental. They will not count on your total score, but they will add to the time given to take the test.

Sample Reading Screens

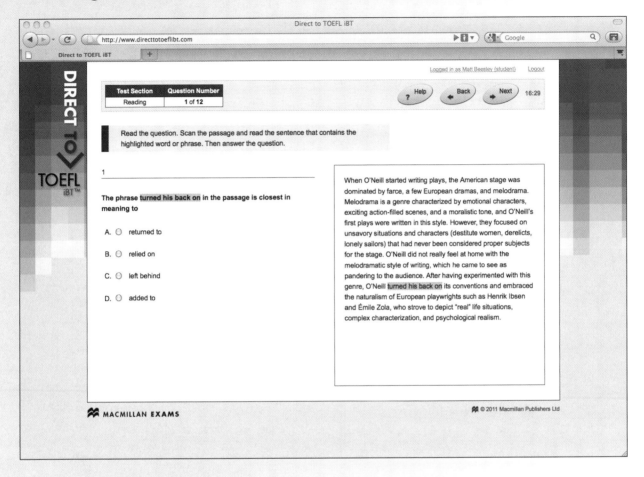

Sample screen shot 1

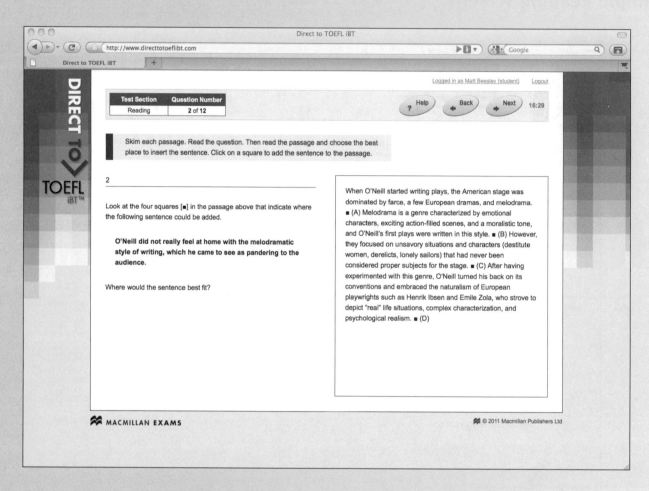

Sample screen shot 2

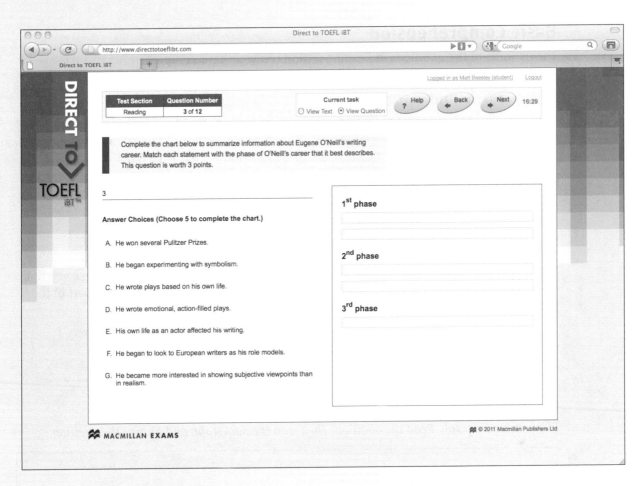

Complete the chart below to summarize information about Eugene O'Neill's writing career. Match each statement with the phase of O'Neill's career that it best describes. This question is worth 3 points.

3 _____

Answer Choices (Choose 5 to complete the chart.)

A. He won several Pulitzer Prizes.

B. He began experimenting with symbolism.

C. He wrote plays based on his own life.

D. He wrote emotional, action-filled plays.

E. His own life as an actor affected his writing.

F. He began to look to European writers as his role models.

G. He became more interested in showing subjective viewpoints than in realism.

1st phase

2nd phase

3rd phase

MACMILLAN EXAMS   © 2011 Macmillan Publishers Ltd

Sample screen shot 3

Skills

Basic Comprehension

The majority of the questions in Reading section test your basic comprehension of a passage by asking you about main ideas and details, or about the writer's purpose.

Skill 1 Factual Information

Each passage has from three to six factual information questions. There are more factual information questions per passage than any other type of question. A factual information question asks you for a specific detail or fact that is explicitly mentioned in the passage.

Examples

> According to paragraph 3, which event happened first?
>
> According to the author, what was the main cause of the Civil War?
>
> Which of the following does the author use to describe Hopi pottery?

You can scan a passage looking for the key words to help you answer a question. Once you find a key word, read several sentences before and after the word to make sure that that part of the passage specifically answers the question.

Tip	Skimming and scanning will save you time and help direct your reading. Review skimming and scanning on pages 16–24.

Practice

Skim each paragraph. Read the question. Then scan the paragraph and answer the question.

1.

At a national level, the first effective campaign to improve worker safety began in the 1880s among railroad workers, who pushed for the development of better brakes and coupling mechanisms for freight cars. This led to improvements that not only increased safety, but productivity as well, and thus were readily accepted by the railroad industry. In 1893, Congress passed the first federal law primarily intended to improve work safety. This was the Safety Appliance Act, which mandated the use of the new equipment.

According to the paragraph, railroad workers demanded

(A) better wages
(B) safer equipment
(C) increased productivity
(D) a new federal law

2.

In 1908, Congress adopted the Federal Employers' Liability Act, which regulated the amount of damages an employee injured in any interstate railroad accident could recover and which also considerably limited employers' defenses. The cost to the employer for a worker fatality rose from roughly $200 to $2,000. Only two years later, New York became the first state to enact a Workmen's Compensation Law. Rather than requiring injured workers to sue their employers and prove the employer was at fault, the law automatically compensated all injuries at predetermined rates. Samuel Gompers, the head of the American Federation of Labor, had studied a similar compensation law in Germany. The law appealed to American businesses because it made costs predictable and reduced labor issues. It appealed to unions and other industry reformers because it promised more predictable benefits. Between 1911 and 1921, forty-four states passed similar laws.

According to the paragraph, New York's Workmen's Compensation Law

(A) applied only to railroad workers

(B) was not acceptable to most business owners

(C) allowed injured workers to sue their employers

(D) determined how much injured workers would be paid

3.

The first of the ways volcanoes form is where an oceanic plate collides with a continental plate. The oceanic plate is the heavier one, and it slides under the lighter continental plate. As the oceanic plate sinks, it heats up and melts. This molten rock, or "magma", is lighter than the solid rock above it. The magma begins to rise and eventually breaks through the surface. The area where an oceanic and a continental plate collide is called a "subduction zone", and it is along this kind of boundary that the volcanoes form in the Ring of Fire in the Pacific. These volcanoes spew dark, heavy lava, the name given to magma once it reaches the surface.

According to the author, where do volcanoes form?

(A) At the boundary of two plates

(B) In an area where rocks are lighter

(C) Beneath the surface of a continental plate

(D) At a place where rocks slide into the ocean

4.

The third main way volcanoes form is by hot spots. For reasons not yet known, magma rises very close to the surface in some locations. The magma builds up under these areas until the pressure causes the crust to rise, usually from the ocean floor. Eventually, a series of volcanoes form in roughly the same spot, some lasting longer than others, until a huge mountain of land is built up. This is the process Kilauea and Mauna Loa on the Island of Hawaii are currently undergoing. Many hot spots are extremely long-lasting, some, such as the one under Hawaii, enduring for millions of years. As the Pacific plate passes over this hot spot, the old island and volcano move northwest, and eventually, enough pressure builds up and a new volcano erupts over the same hot spot but under a new piece of land. All the Hawaiian Islands were formed this way. To the northwest of the Hawaiian Islands are older islands formed at this same hot spot, islands that have weathered away and are no longer visible from the surface.

According to the paragraph, which of the following is true about hot spots?

(A) They erupt infrequently.

(B) They are constantly moving.

(C) They form islands in the ocean.

(D) They are extremely short-lived.

Skill 2 Vocabulary

Each passage has from three to five vocabulary questions. After factual information questions, there are more vocabulary questions per passage than any other type of question. A vocabulary question asks you to give a synonym for a word or a paraphrase for a phrase.

Examples

The word climatic in paragraph 3 is closest in meaning to

By describing bears as omnivores, the author means

Use the context to help you understand the meaning of the word. Be especially careful with words that can have more than one meaning. You must choose the meaning of the word in the context of the passage. The answer choices will all be the same part of speech as the highlighted vocabulary word, and the tense or number will also be the same.

Tip	Substitute the word you think is the correct answer in the sentence to see if it makes sense.

Practice

Read the question. Scan the passage and read the sentence that contains the highlighted word or phrase. Then answer the question.

1.

When O'Neill started writing plays, the American stage was dominated by farce, a few European dramas, and melodrama. Melodrama is a genre characterized by emotional characters, exciting action-filled scenes, and a moralistic tone, and O'Neill's first plays were written in this style. However, they focused on unsavory situations and characters (destitute women, derelicts, lonely sailors) that had never been considered proper subjects for the stage. O'Neill did not really feel at home with the melodramatic style of writing, which he came to see as pandering to the audience. After having experimented with this genre, O'Neill turned his back on its conventions and embraced the naturalism of European playwrights, such as Henrik Ibsen and Émile Zola, who strove to depict "real" life situations, complex characterization, and psychological realism.

The phrase turned his back on in the passage is closest in meaning to

- (A) returned to
- (B) relied on
- (C) left behind
- (D) added to

2.

In the latter part of O'Neill's writing career, he rejected pure expressionism and the most highly theatrical tone of his previous devices, returning to naturalism while retaining a subtler form of symbolism. During this period, he produced his most celebrated and fully-developed work. In particular, he honed his skills at depicting realistic, psychological close-ups of his characters.

The word celebrated in the passage is closest in meaning to

- (A) famous
- (B) rewarded
- (C) enjoyable
- (D) professional

3.

In both these traditional cultures, visual art is created on the ground for ritual use; both cultures consider the artwork to have life and power; both cultures integrate the visual art with dance and song and stories; and both cultures destroy the images at the end of the ceremonies. Contrasting with cultures rooted in Western Europe, religion in these cultures is not separate from daily life, visual art is not separate from other arts, such as music and dance, and art is not a commodity created for consumers.

The word integrate in the passage is closest in meaning to

(A) consider

(B) separate

(C) value

(D) combine

4.

The Navajos (who also refer to themselves as Diné) use sand painting in extensive rituals called "sings". Sings are ceremonies that involve many relatives and friends and are intended to bless, protect, or heal the individual for whom they are held. Sand painting plays a central role in the ceremony, but singing and dancing are also included. A design specific to the particular ritual is painted with sand, charcoal, pollen, and clay on the ground inside the hogan. The images portray mountains and other features of the region, the gods who created them, and legends and stories from the past. The sand painting is considered a living being: when the "patient" lies on the image, the power of the gods is absorbed, and harmony is restored within his or her life. When the ritual is completed, the sand and other elements are returned to the earth.

The word restored in the passage is closest in meaning to

(A) contained

(B) returned

(C) protected

(D) maintained

Skill 3 Negative

Each passage has from zero to two negative questions. A negative question asks you to determine which of the answer choices is NOT true.

Tip	The words *not* and *except* are in capital letters in these questions. When you see NOT or EXCEPT, read the question carefully to make sure you understand.

Examples

According to the passage, which of the following is NOT true?

The author discusses all of the following reasons EXCEPT:

A negative question may be based on information in one paragraph, or it may be based on information in the entire passage. The correct answer to a negative question is the choice that is NOT mentioned or is NOT true.

Practice

Skim each passage. Read the question. Then read the passage and answer the question.

1.

In 1908, Congress adopted the Federal Employers' Liability Act, which regulated the amount of damages an employee injured in any interstate railroad accident could recover, and which also considerably limited employers' defenses. The cost to the employer for a worker fatality rose from roughly $200 to $2,000. Only two years later, New York became the first state to enact a Workmen's Compensation Law. Rather than requiring injured workers to sue their employers and prove the employer was at fault, the law automatically compensated all injuries at predetermined rates. Samuel Gompers, the head of the American Federation of Labor, had studied a similar compensation law in Germany. The law appealed to American businesses because it made costs predictable and reduced labor issues. It appealed to unions and other industry reformers because it promised more predictable benefits. Between 1911 and 1921, forty-four states passed similar laws.

According to the paragraph, all of the following are true about New York's Workmen's Compensation Law EXCEPT that:

(A) It satisfied both business and labor leaders.

(B) It was similar to a law already in effect in Germany.

(C) It compensated injured workers without the need to go to court.

(D) It was the only such law in the United States for several decades.

2.

As accident costs rose between World Wars I and II, the safety record of American industry steadily improved. Separately, changes in technology and labor markets also contributed to an increased safety record. During the Great Depression of the 1930s, job turnover was relatively low. This meant there were fewer new employees, who were the ones more likely to get hurt. The spread of electrical lighting in factories also reduced injuries. The economic boom and the entry of many new workers during World War II led to another rise in industrial injuries. However, that declined again after 1945, particularly as labor unions increasingly focused on worker safety.

According to the paragraph, which of the following is NOT true?
(A) People changed jobs frequently during the Great Depression.
(B) There was an increase in worker injuries during World War II.
(C) One factor contributing to a safer workplace was increased use of electric lights.
(D) Technological advances improved workplace safety between World Wars I and II.

3.

Our planet is made up of several layers. The thin outer layer of the surface supports life. This section of the globe, the crust, is cool enough for molten rock to harden. Processes such as weathering and erosion transform the hardened rock into dirt, which through the interaction and eventual decay of living plants and animals forms soil. The crust is also cool enough for water, originally produced from volcanic explosions, to condense into rain, rivers, and oceans. Below this crust, we know, is another layer of hotter, flexible rock that stretches and deforms. The crust floats on this plastic layer. Below that layer is a thick layer of flowing and swirling molten rock, where temperatures reach thousands of degrees Celsius. Below that is the core. Because the crust is essentially frozen rock, it is brittle and breaks and shifts with the movements of the layer below. The crust is broken up into sections called plates, and as these plates move, they bump into each other along their boundaries. The collisions of plates can lead to the formation of volcanoes.

The passage mentions all of the following EXCEPT:
(A) differences between the layers
(B) where water comes from
(C) how rock becomes soil
(D) the temperature of the core

4.

If two plates run into each other, then somewhere else, plates must move away from each other. The second type of volcano occurs as a result of spreading along the middle of the ocean floors. As the crust thins when the plates separate, new, molten rock rises to the surface, and it often forms volcanoes. Much of the Mid-Atlantic Ridge is a series of vents and volcanoes under the ocean. The ridge is entirely underwater, except for the volcanoes of Iceland. The north-south axis of Iceland is marked by cracks, called *vents* or *fissures*, where the nearly constant volcanic activity is visible on the surface.

According to the paragraph, all of the following are true about Iceland's volcanoes EXCEPT that:

   (A) They are still very active.
   (B) They are located where two plates collide.
   (C) They formed at a place where the Earth's crust thinned.
   (D) They are part of a mountain chain that is mostly under the ocean.

Skill 4   Inference

Each passage has from zero to two inference questions. An inference question asks you to make a judgment on something not directly stated in the passage.

Examples

   The author of the passage implies that

   Which of the following can be inferred about Benjamin Franklin?

   The description of oil drilling in paragraph 2 implies that

Your answer choice is not a guess. It is a logical judgment based on information given in the passage. Rather than identifying facts, you will have to interpret their meaning.

Tip When you see the verbs *imply* or *infer* in a question, you will need to make an inference. The answer will not be stated directly anywhere.

Practice

Skim each passage. Read the question. Then read the passage and answer the question.

1.

Only limited statistical data exist concerning the safety of American mills and factories prior to 1870. What is known is that employers tended to have only minimal interest in workplace safety. Because of that, American industry developed production methods that were both highly profitable and often extremely hazardous. Following the Civil War, with its great loss of life, many young and very inexperienced workers entered the job market. The factories where they found work were filled with dangerous machines driven by a jumble of overhead belts, pulleys, and gears. The air workers breathed was filled with toxic substances, and tragic fires were a frequent occurrence. Reports from various state labor bureaus in the 1870s described workplace tragedies, some quite grisly, which led early social reformers to call for state governments to enact factory safety and health laws. In 1877, Massachusetts became the first state to pass a factory inspection law which required guarding belts, shafts, and gears; protection on elevators; and adequate fire exits. Other states followed suit.

What can be inferred about the reasons for an inexperienced workforce following the Civil War?

(A) Many of the experienced workers had died during the war.

(B) Workers lacked experience because of military duty during the war.

(C) Experienced workers did not want to work with dangerous machines.

(D) Employers did not want to pay the higher wages demanded by experienced workers.

2.

The Navajos (who also refer to themselves as Diné) use sand painting in extensive rituals called "sings". Sings are ceremonies that involve many relatives and friends and are intended to bless, protect, or heal the individual for whom they are held. Sand painting plays a central role in the ceremony, but singing and dancing are also included. A design specific to the particular ritual is painted with sand, charcoal, pollen, and clay on the ground inside the hogan. The images portray mountains and other features of the region, the gods who created them, and legends and stories from the past. The sand painting is considered a living being: when the "patient" lies on the image, the power of the gods is absorbed, and harmony is restored within his or her life. When the ritual is completed, the sand and other elements are returned to the earth.

What can be inferred about the Navajos' sand painting designs?

(A) Most are bright and colorful.

(B) They always depict dancing and singing.

(C) The same designs are used repeatedly.

(D) The sand paintings are kept and reused.

3.

When O'Neill started writing plays, the American stage was dominated by farce, a few European dramas, and melodrama. Melodrama is a genre characterized by emotional characters, exciting action-filled scenes, and a moralistic tone, and O'Neill's first plays were written in this style. However, they focused on unsavory situations and characters (destitute women, derelicts, lonely sailors) that had never been considered proper subjects for the stage. O'Neill did not really feel at home with the melodramatic style of writing, which he came to see as pandering to the audience. After having experimented with this genre, O'Neill turned his back on its conventions and embraced the naturalism of European playwrights, such as Henrik Ibsen and Émile Zola, who strove to depict "real" life situations, complex characterization, and psychological realism.

O'Neill's early plays, which include the Pulitzer Prize-winner *Anna Christie*, are often called the "sea plays" because most are set near or on the sea. Eschewing melodramatic conventions, O'Neill asked audiences to identify with desperate people and other morally ambiguous characters. Often, good characters ended badly; not only had O'Neill created a new kind of American naturalism, he had created America's first tragedies.

Which of the following can be inferred about O'Neill's writing?

(A) He followed the conventions of his times.

(B) He preferred realism to melodrama.

(C) His plays generally had happy endings.

(D) His characters had high morals.

4.

Mining his unhappy childhood for themes and characters, he wrote his most autobiographical plays: *Long Day's Journey into Night*, *The Iceman Cometh*, and *Moon for The Misbegotten*. These plays are notable for their length and repetition of themes and ideas.

These plays show O'Neill bringing together his previous themes in powerful and haunting ways. *Long Day's Journey into Night*, generally regarded as his best play, brings together several lost souls in the same family. As in previous plays, these characters' pipe dreams are the only way they can sustain themselves in a hostile world. The mother is a drug addict, the father is a failed actor who has spent his life compromising his ideals in favor of gratifying the audience's tastes, the older son is a bitter alcoholic, and the younger son is a disillusioned invalid. Over the course of one day, the members of the family lose their pipe dreams and struggle to find some sense of purpose in their lives. It is in these later plays, and especially *Long Day's Journey into Night*, that O'Neill finally found the dramatic form that expressed his inner vision.

What does the author imply about O'Neill's family?

(A) O'Neill's relatives shared many of his ideas.

(B) Drug and alcohol problems plagued the O'Neill family.

(C) Many of O'Neill's relatives were involved in the theater.

(D) The family was extremely supportive of O'Neill's work.

Skill 5   Purpose

Each passage has from zero to two purpose questions. A purpose question asks you to determine *why* information was included in the passage.

Examples

> The author of the passage details planting methods because
>
> Why does the author mention the Great Lakes?
>
> The author discusses new technology in paragraph 3 so that

Be careful about words that introduce reasons, such as *to provide, to argue, to criticize, to note*. These may be used in the answer choices to distract you. Read carefully and look throughout the passage for statements that provide a reason.

Tip	This type of question can be challenging because the reasons are not expressly stated in the passage. You may have to analyze information in multiple sentences in order to arrive at the purpose.

Practice

Skim each passage. Read the question. Then read the passage and answer the question.

1.

Only two years later, New York became the first state to enact a Workmen's Compensation Law. Rather than requiring injured workers to sue their employers and prove the employer was at fault, the law automatically compensated all injuries at predetermined rates. Samuel Gompers, the head of the American Federation of Labor, had studied a similar compensation law in Germany. The law appealed to American businesses because it made costs predictable and reduced labor issues. It appealed to unions and other industry reformers because it promised more predictable benefits. Between 1911 and 1921, forty-four states passed similar laws.

The author mentions that Samuel Gompers studied a German law in order to

(A) illustrate how well-educated labor leaders were

(B) contrast German labor laws with American labor laws

(C) argue that Germany was ahead of the United States in safety standards

(D) show that labor unions supported the new Workmen's Compensation Law

2.

By 1968, safety standards were again slipping. Each year more than 14,000 workers were killed and 2.2 million were injured on the job. President Lyndon Johnson cited inadequate standards, lagging research, and a patchwork of ineffective federal laws when he called on Congress to enact a comprehensive new job-safety and health program. The proposed legislation failed in committee, however, and never came to a vote.

Why does the author mention the numbers of workers killed and injured?

(A) To support the statement that safety standards were getting worse

(B) To compare safety standards in 1968 to previous years

(C) To show how many workers were benefiting from federal laws

(D) To explain why President Johnson's legislation failed in committee

3.

Aboriginal art is rooted in Dreamtime, the time when ancestor spirits dreamed the earth and its inhabitants into being. Dreamtime, unlike ordinary chronological time, exists simultaneously in the past, present, and future. Aboriginal clans in Australia employ ritual activities to access Dreamtime and the power found in specific places. Ground art, songs, and dance enact and bring into present-day experience the ancestral spirits who created the local animals, plants, and rock formations, as well as events in the clan's past, such as successful hunts and the discovery of water sources.

Why does the author discuss the aboriginal concept of Dreamtime?
- (A) To contrast it with everyday aboriginal life
- (B) To give an example of a traditional aboriginal belief
- (C) To explain the reasons behind certain aboriginal rituals
- (D) To describe an important time in the aboriginal calendar

4.

If two plates run into each other, then somewhere else, plates must move away from each other. The second type of volcano occurs as a result of spreading along the middle of the ocean floors. As the crust thins when the plates separate, new, molten rock rises to the surface, and it often forms volcanoes. Much of the Mid-Atlantic Ridge is a series of vents and volcanoes under the ocean. The ridge is entirely underwater, except for the volcanoes of Iceland. The north-south axis of Iceland is marked by cracks, called vents or fissures, where the nearly constant volcanic activity is visible on the surface.

Why does the author mention the Mid-Atlantic Ridge?
- (A) To explain how Iceland was formed
- (B) To contrast its volcanoes with those of Iceland
- (C) To describe what is beneath the Atlantic Ocean
- (D) To give an example of what results when plates separate

Skill 6   Reference
Each passage has from zero to two reference questions. A reference question asks you to determine the noun or noun phrase that a pronoun refers to. The pronoun will be highlighted in the passage.

Examples
The word them in paragraph 3 refers to
Which in paragraph 2 refers to

Tip	Many of these questions ask about the referent for the pronouns *it* and *they*. Remember that *who* (for people) and *which* (for things) are also types of pronouns.

The noun that the pronoun refers to should match the referenced word in number. For example, if you are asked about *they*, scan for plural nouns in that sentence and the sentences just before and after. Subsitute the noun you think is the correct answer to see if it makes sense.

Practice

Read the question. Scan the passage and read the sentence that contains the highlighted word. Then answer the question.

1.

Following the Civil War, with its great loss of life, many young and very inexperienced workers entered the job market. The factories where they found work were filled with dangerous machines driven by a jumble of overhead belts, pulleys, and gears. The air workers breathed was filled with toxic substances, and tragic fires were a frequent occurrence. Reports from various state labor bureaus in the 1870s described workplace tragedies, some quite grisly, which led early social reformers to call for state governments to enact factory safety and health laws. In 1877, Massachusetts became the first state to pass a factory inspection law which required guarding belts, shafts, and gears; protection on elevators; and adequate fire exits. Other states followed suit.

The word which in the passage refers to

(A) state labor bureaus
(B) pulleys and gears
(C) workplace tragedies
(D) dangerous machines

2.

When O'Neill started writing plays, the American stage was dominated by farce, a few European dramas, and melodrama. Melodrama is a genre characterized by emotional characters, exciting action-filled scenes, and a moralistic tone, and O'Neill's first plays were written in this style. However, they focused on unsavory situations and characters (destitute women, derelicts, lonely sailors) that had never been considered proper subjects for the stage.

The word they in the passage refers to

(A) melodramas
(B) European dramas
(C) action-filled scenes
(D) O'Neill's first plays

3.

While traditional Navajos have very different gods and belief structures from those held by Australian aboriginal clans, they too have no separation between religious and secular worlds. Navajos also have ancestral beings or gods ("the Holy People") that were active in creating specific local natural features. In addition, Navajos also believe that the sacred beings are active and involved in the daily life of the people.

The word they in the passage refers to

  (A) traditional Navajos
  (B) aboriginal clans
  (C) different gods
  (D) belief structures

4.

Our planet is made up of several layers. The thin outer layer of the surface supports life. This section of the globe, the crust, is cool enough for molten rock to harden. Processes such as weathering and erosion transform the hardened rock into dirt, which, through the interaction and eventual decay of living plants and animals, forms soil.

The word which in the passage refers to

  (A) globe
  (B) crust
  (C) rock
  (D) dirt

Skill 7   Simplification

Each passage has either one simplification question or none. A simplification question asks you to recognize an exact paraphrase of a sentence.

Example

Which of the following best expresses the information in the highlighted sentence?

The paraphrase must not change the meaning of the original sentence, and it will not leave out important information. The correct answer is another way of saying the same thing as the passage sentence. Make sure you understand the meaning of the highlighted sentence. Then look for the answer choice that has the same meaning.

Tip   Try to eliminate one or two answer choices right away. The easiest ones to eliminate will be those that change the meaning in some way.

Practice

Skim each passage. Read the question. Then read the passage and answer the question.

1.

Following the Civil War, with its great loss of life, many young and very inexperienced workers entered the job market. The factories where they found work were filled with dangerous machines driven by a jumble of overhead belts, pulleys, and gears. The air workers breathed was filled with toxic substances, and tragic fires were a frequent occurrence. Reports from various state labor bureaus in the 1870s described workplace tragedies, some quite grisly, which led early social reformers to call for state governments to enact factory safety and health laws. In 1877, Massachusetts became the first state to pass a factory inspection law which required guarding belts, shafts, and gears; protection on elevators; and adequate fire exits. Other states followed suit.

Which of the following sentences best expresses the information in the highlighted sentence?

(A) State labor bureaus led the way toward reform of safety and health laws during the 1870s.

(B) Because of reports of terrible workplace accidents, social reformers in the 1870s called for safety and health laws.

(C) In the 1870s, state labor bureaus had the job of reporting workplace accidents to government law enforcers.

(D) During the 1870s, the responsibility for enacting safety and health laws was moved from labor bureaus to the government.

2.

At a national level, the first effective campaign to improve worker safety began in the 1880s among railroad workers, who pushed for the development of better brakes and coupling mechanisms for freight cars. This led to improvements that not only increased safety, but productivity as well and thus were readily accepted by the railroad industry. In 1893, Congress passed the first federal law primarily intended to improve work safety. This was the Safety Appliance Act, which mandated the use of the new equipment.

Which of the following sentences best expresses the information in the highlighted sentence?

(A) The railroad industry led the way to increased safety and productivity.

(B) The railroad industry accepted only those improvements which increased productivity.

(C) The railroad industry accepted the safety improvements because they also improved productivity.

(D) When workers started producing more, the railroad industry accepted their request for safety improvements.

3.

Mauna Loa volcano in Hawaii continually boils over with lava, the red-hot liquid rock oozing down the mountainside until it flows into the Pacific, sending up steam as it mixes with the ocean waters. Mount St. Helens exploded in a billowing cloud of ash and steam, blowing an entire mountaintop into the air. Volcanologists have braved molten lava flows and poisonous gases to study the birth and behavior of these powerful natural phenomena up close.

Which of the following sentences best expresses the information in the highlighted sentence?

(A) Scientists have put themselves in dangerous situations in order to study volcanoes in action.

(B) Only brave scientists dare to climb volcanoes to study them while they are active.

(C) Volcanologists are scientists who study the formation of volcanoes from lava and poisonous gases.

(D) It is a powerful, though dangerous, experience to study the action of a volcano up close.

4.

The third main way volcanoes form is by hot spots. For reasons not yet known, magma rises very close to the surface in some locations. The magma builds up under these areas until the pressure causes the crust to rise, usually from the ocean floor. Eventually, a series of volcanoes form in roughly the same spot, some lasting longer than others, until a huge mountain of land is built up. This is the process Kilauea and Mauna Loa on the Island of Hawaii are currently undergoing. Many hot spots are extremely long-lasting, some, such as the one under Hawaii, enduring for millions of years. As the Pacific plate passes over this hot spot, the old island and volcano move northwest, and eventually, enough pressure builds up and a new volcano erupts over the same hot spot, but under a new piece of land. All the Hawaiian Islands were formed this way. To the northwest of the Hawaiian Islands are older islands formed at this same hot spot, islands that have weathered away and are no longer visible from the surface.

Which of the following sentences best expresses the information in the highlighted sentence?

(A) As a new volcano erupts, a new piece of land is formed over the old island and volcano.

(B) The Pacific plate moves over the hot spot, causing the volcano to erupt, and this pushes the old island away.

(C) The pressure of the hot spot eventually pushes the old island and volcano away, making room for the formation of new land.

(D) The movement of the Pacific plate causes the volcanic island to move away from the hot spot, and a new island forms in its old place.

Skill 8 Text Insertion

Each passage has only one text insertion question or none. A text insertion question asks you to place a sentence in the appropriate spot in the passage. On your computer screen, the passage will have four black squares. You will choose the best place to insert the new sentence.

Example

Where would this sentence best fit?

This type of question tests your ability to understand the way a passage is organized. Understanding how transition words and phrases connect ideas will help you place the sentence. The sentence must fit logically in its new position.

Transition words	
As a result	In other words
Consequently	On the other hand
For example	Therefore
Furthermore	In conclusion

Tip	Read the paragraph to yourself with the sentence in the spot you think is correct to see if it makes sense.

Practice

Skim each passage. Read the question. Then read the passage and choose the best place to insert the sentence.

1.

When O'Neill started writing plays, the American stage was dominated by farce, a few European dramas, and melodrama. ■ **(A)** Melodrama is a genre characterized by emotional characters, exciting action-filled scenes, and a moralistic tone, and O'Neill's first plays were written in this style. ■ **(B)** However, they focused on unsavory situations and characters (destitute women, derelicts, lonely sailors) that had never been considered proper subjects for the stage. ■ **(C)** After having experimented with this genre, O'Neill turned his back on its conventions and embraced the naturalism of European playwrights such as Henrik Ibsen and Émile Zola, who strove to depict "real" life situations, complex characterization, and psychological realism. ■ **(D)**

Look at the four squares [■] in the passage above that indicate where the following sentence could be added.

O'Neill did not really feel at home with the melodramatic style of writing, which he came to see as pandering to the audience.

Where would the sentence best fit?

2.

O'Neill's early plays, which include the Pulitzer Prize-winner *Anna Christie*, are often called the "sea plays" because most are set near or on the sea. ■ **(A)** Eschewing melodramatic conventions, O'Neill asked audiences to identify with desperate people and other morally ambiguous characters. ■ **(B)** Often, good characters ended badly; not only had O'Neill created a new kind of American naturalism, he had created America's first tragedies. ■ **(C)** The sea plays also show the first glimpses of topics that O'Neill would return to again and again in his writing. ■ **(D)**

Look at the four squares [■] in the passage above that indicate where the following sentence could be added.

These were themes such as the search for identity and meaning in life, familial disintegration, and the conflict of idealism and materialism.

Where would the sentence best fit?

3.

When a nomadic Australian aboriginal clan comes to a new site, they gather for a ground art ritual. ■ **(A)** Clan members create designs with different colored sand, feathers, plants, stones and other objects. ■ **(B)** These rituals are normally secret; the songs, dances, and designs have power and are intended only for clan members. Through reenacting the creation myths and clan history associated with the given area, cultural beliefs, as well as knowledge useful for survival are passed from one generation to the next. ■ **(C)** When the ritual is completed, the painting is scattered. ■ **(D)**

Look at the four squares [■] in the passage above that indicate where the following sentence could be added.

Many of the designs are essentially "maps", with symbols referring to specific features of the local landscape and also events that occurred there in Dreamtime.

Where would the sentence best fit?

4.

■ **(A)** Both of these cultures, however, have been influenced by western European cultures. ■ **(B)** In modern times, individual artists in both cultures have adapted traditional designs for permanent art to be sold to outsiders. Navajo weavers now incorporate sand painting designs into their blankets, and other Navajo artists create permanent sand paintings by gluing the colored sand onto various backings. ■ **(C)** Modern-day Australian aboriginal artists also use designs that resemble their traditional ground art in paintings made with sand or with paint. ■ **(D)** Like Navajo artists, they alter the prescribed ritual designs, keeping the exact ritualistic patterns secret to their clan.

Look at the four squares [■] in the passage above that indicate where the following sentence could be added.

Most Navajo artists alter the design somewhat to avoid a curse from the "Holy People" for use of the designs outside of prescribed rituals.

Where would the sentence best fit?

Reading to Learn

Skill 9 Summary

Each passage has either one summary question or one completion question (see Skill 10). A *summary question* asks you to pick three major ideas in a passage to complete a chart. You will be given six answer choices, but only three are correct. Some options are details and will not be used.

Tip	When you first read through the answer choices, look for more general statements. As you read the passage and locate one of the answers, add it to the chart.

Example

Complete the summary by choosing THREE answer options that represent the main ideas in the passage.

You must be able to organize the author's main points and distinguish the major ideas from the minor ideas. This type of question is worth up to 2 points. If you get all three correct, you receive 2 points; two correct, 1 point; one or none correct, no points.

Practice

Skim each passage. Read the question and answer choices. Then read the passage and complete the chart.

1.

The Rise of Safety Standards in the American Workplace

Only limited statistical data exist concerning the safety of American mills and factories prior to 1870. What is known is that employers tended to have only minimal interest in workplace safety. Because of that, American industry developed production methods that were both highly profitable and often extremely hazardous. Following the Civil War, with its great loss of life, many young and very inexperienced workers entered the job market. The factories where they found work were filled with dangerous machines driven by a jumble of overhead belts, pulleys, and gears. The air workers breathed was filled with toxic substances, and tragic fires were a frequent occurrence. Reports from various state labor bureaus in the 1870s described workplace tragedies, some quite grisly, which led early social reformers to call for state governments to enact factory safety and health laws. In 1877, Massachusetts became the first state to pass a factory inspection law which required guarding belts, shafts, and gears; protection on elevators; and adequate fire exits. Other states followed suit.

At a national level, the first effective campaign to improve worker safety began in the 1880s among railroad workers, who pushed for the development of better brakes and coupling mechanisms for freight cars. This led to improvements that not only increased safety, but productivity as well and thus were readily accepted by the railroad industry. In 1893, Congress passed the first federal law primarily intended to improve work safety. This was the Safety Appliance Act, which mandated the use of the new equipment.

Although a worker injured on the job, or his/her heirs, could sue an employer for compensation, prevailing in court was difficult. Courts usually denied liability if the employer could show that the worker had assumed the risk, had been partly at fault, or had been injured due to the actions of another employee. Based on surveys taken around 1900, only about half the families of workers fatally injured on the job recovered anything, and the average compensation was equal to only about six months' pay.

In 1908, Congress adopted the Federal Employers' Liability Act, which regulated the amount of damages an employee injured in any interstate railroad accident could recover and which also considerably limited employers' defenses. The cost to the employer for a worker fatality rose from roughly $200 to $2,000. Only two years later, New York became the first state to enact a Workmen's Compensation Law. Rather than requiring injured workers to sue their employers and prove the employer was at fault, the law automatically compensated all injuries at predetermined rates. Samuel Gompers, the head of the American Federation of Labor, had studied a similar compensation law in Germany. The law appealed to American businesses because it made costs predictable and reduced labor issues. It appealed to unions and other industry reformers because it promised more predictable benefits. Between 1911 and 1921, forty-four states passed similar laws.

As accident costs rose between World Wars I and II, the safety record of American industry steadily improved. Separately, changes in technology and labor markets also contributed to an increased safety record. During the Great Depression of the 1930s, job turnover was relatively low. This meant there were fewer new employees, who were the ones more likely to get hurt. The spread of electrical lighting in factories also reduced injuries. The economic boom and the entry of many new workers during World War II led to another rise in industrial injuries. However, that declined again after 1945, particularly as labor unions increasingly focused on worker safety.

By 1968, safety standards were again slipping. Each year more than 14,000 workers were killed and 2.2 million were injured on the job. President Lyndon Johnson cited inadequate standards, lagging research, and a patchwork of ineffective federal laws when he called on Congress to enact a comprehensive new job-safety and health program. The proposed legislation failed in committee, however, and never came to a vote.

Despite such setbacks, the idea of a comprehensive job-safety and health program was far from defeated. With labor leaders and the business community at considerable odds, a bitter legislative struggle ensued. At length, through grassroots efforts and the introduction of various amendments, a compromise was reached and in 1970, President Richard Nixon signed the Williams-Steiger Occupational Safety and Health Act. This act finally gave the federal government the authority to create and enforce uniform safety and health standards for most of America's workers.

Question

An introductory sentence for a summary of the passage is given below. Complete the summary by choosing THREE answers that best represent the main ideas in the passage. This question is worth 2 points.

Safety standards in the American workplace have steadily improved over the last century and a half.

- _____

- _____

- _____

Answer Choices

(A) During the last quarter of the nineteenth century, the government began paying attention to safety conditions in the workplace.

(B) Railroad workers were among the first to call for safer conditions in the workplace.

(C) Legislation in the early twentieth century made it easier for workers to get compensation for on-the-job injuries, while technological advances improved the level of safety.

(D) The electric lighting systems in use during the Great Depression were not nearly as safe as those in use today, and this caused many workplace injuries.

(E) President Johnson brought attention to the fact that the safety standards in existence during his time in office were not adequate.

(F) Because of legislation enacted during Nixon's presidency, the U.S. government is now empowered to regulate health and safety standards throughout the country.

2.

Formation of Volcanoes

Mauna Loa volcano in Hawaii continually boils over with lava, the red-hot liquid rock oozing down the mountainside until it flows into the Pacific, sending up steam as it mixes with the ocean waters. Mount St. Helens exploded in a billowing cloud of ash and steam, blowing an entire mountaintop into the air. Volcanologists have braved molten lava flows and poisonous gases to study the birth and behavior of these powerful natural phenomena up close.

Our planet is made up of several layers. The thin outer layer of the surface supports life. This section of the globe, the crust, is cool enough for molten rock to harden. Processes such as weathering and erosion transform the hardened rock into dirt, which, through the interaction and eventual decay of living plants and animals, forms soil. The crust is also cool enough for water, originally produced from volcanic explosions, to condense into rain, rivers, and oceans. Below this crust, we know, is another layer of hotter, flexible rock that stretches and deforms. The crust floats on this plastic layer. Below that layer is a thick layer of flowing and swirling molten rock, where temperatures reach thousands of degrees Celsius. Below that is the core. Because the crust is essentially frozen rock, it is brittle and breaks and shifts with the movements of the layer below. The crust is broken up into sections called plates, and as these plates move, they bump into each other along their boundaries. The collisions of plates can lead to the formation of volcanoes.

The first of the ways volcanoes form is where an oceanic plate collides with a continental plate. The oceanic plate is the heavier one, and it slides under the lighter continental plate. As the oceanic plate sinks, it heats up and melts. This molten rock, or "magma", is lighter than the solid rock above it. The magma begins to rise and eventually breaks through the surface. The area where an oceanic and a continental plate collide is called a subduction zone, and it is along this kind of boundary that the volcanoes form in the Ring of Fire in the Pacific. These volcanoes spew dark, heavy lava, the name given to magma once it reaches the surface.

If two plates run into each other, then somewhere else, plates must move away from each other. The second type of volcano occurs as a result of spreading along the middle of the ocean floors. As the crust thins when the plates separate, new, molten rock rises to the surface, and it often forms volcanoes. Much of the Mid-Atlantic Ridge is a series of vents and volcanoes under the ocean. The ridge is entirely underwater, except for the volcanoes of Iceland. The north-south axis of Iceland is marked by cracks, called vents or fissures, where the nearly constant volcanic activity is visible on the surface.

The third main way volcanoes form is by hot spots. For reasons not yet known, magma rises very close to the surface in some locations. The magma builds up under these areas until the pressure causes the crust to rise, usually from the ocean floor. Eventually, a series of volcanoes form in roughly the same spot, some lasting longer than others, until a huge mountain of land is built up. This is the process Kilauea and Mauna Loa on the Island of Hawaii are currently undergoing. Many hot spots are extremely long lasting, some, such as the one under Hawaii, enduring for millions of years. As the Pacific plate passes over this hot spot, the old island and volcano move northwest, and eventually, enough pressure builds up and a new volcano erupts over the same hot spot but under a new piece of land. All the Hawaiian Islands were formed this way. To the northwest of the Hawaiian Islands are older islands formed at this same hot spot, islands that have weathered away and are no longer visible from the surface.

Volcanoes form when this thin layer of brittle crust on the outside of the planet cracks or stretches thin enough for the hot liquid rock underneath the crust to force its way out through the surface. Volcanoes give us a glimpse of what is going on below the surface of our planet, right beneath our feet.

Question

An introductory sentence for a brief summary of the passage is given below. Complete the summary by choosing THREE answers that best represent the main ideas in the passage. This question is worth 2 points.

Volcanoes form on the Earth's surface in several different ways.

- _____
- _____
- _____

Answer Choices

(A) The lava from volcanoes can cause the ocean to steam or blow the top off a mountain.

(B) The Earth's crust is hard and brittle, but the layers beneath it are flexible and shifting.

(C) As the plates in the crust move, volcanoes form where the plates collide and diverge.

(D) Oceanic plates sink below continental plates because they are heavier.

(E) Volcanoes form over hot spots, where a buildup of rising magma bursts through the surface.

(F) The Hawaiian Islands were formed by the Pacific Plate moving over a hot spot in the ocean.

Skill 10 Completion

Each passage has either one completion question or one summary question (see Skill 9).
A *completion question* asks you to complete a chart with ideas from the passage. Some options are not correct and will not be used.

Examples

Complete the chart to summarize information about the two [*events*].

Match the answer choices to the type of mining to which they relate.

Complete the chart by indicating which answers describe dolphins and which answers describe whales.

You can earn up to 3 points for charts with five correct answers, and up to 4 points for charts with seven correct answers. The question will indicate the total point value and may often remind you how many answers will NOT be used.

Tip | You will receive partial credit, so make sure you choose an answer for each bullet (•) in the chart. Don't leave anything blank.

The organization of the passages is usually one of these types:

Classification

Comparison and Contrast

Cause and Effect

Problem and Solution

This kind of question asks you to choose important ideas about the passage and classify them in some way that is related to the organization of the passage.

Practice

Skim each passage. Read the question and answer choices. Then read the passage and complete the chart.

1.

Eugene O'Neill: America's First Great Playwright

Eugene O'Neill (1888–1953) is regarded as America's first great playwright and the first to use drama for literary purposes. He received four Pulitzer Prizes and is the only American playwright to have received a Nobel Prize in Literature (in 1936). Although he is known primarily for his later family tragedies, O'Neill's career as a playwright went through several stylistic phases that demonstrate his constant struggle to find effective means of dramatic expression.

When O'Neill started writing plays, the American stage was dominated by farce, a few European dramas, and melodrama. Melodrama is a genre characterized by emotional characters, exciting action-filled scenes, and a moralistic tone, and O'Neill's first plays were written in this style. However, they focused on unsavory situations and characters (destitute women, derelicts, lonely sailors) that had never been considered proper subjects for the stage. O'Neill did not really feel at home with the melodramatic style of writing, which he came to see as pandering to the audience. After having experimented with this genre, O'Neill turned his back on its conventions and embraced the naturalism of European playwrights, such as Henrik Ibsen and Émile Zola, who strove to depict "real" life situations, complex characterization, and psychological realism.

O'Neill's early plays, which include the Pulitzer Prize-winner *Anna Christie*, are often called the "sea plays" because most are set near or on the sea. Eschewing melodramatic conventions, O'Neill asked audiences to identify with desperate people and other morally ambiguous characters. Often, good characters ended badly; not only had O'Neill created a new kind of American naturalism, he had created America's first tragedies. The sea plays also show the first glimpses of themes O'Neill would return to again and again: characters' search for identity and meaning in life, familial disintegration, and the conflict of idealism and materialism.

In his second phase, O'Neill did not abandon naturalism altogether, but experimented extensively with a wide variety of theatrical devices, using dance, pantomime, symbolic masks and costumes, mythological plots (as in the Greek-inspired *Mourning Becomes Electra*) and Shakespearean conventions such as monologues and asides to the audience (as in the Pulitzer Prize-winning *Strange Interlude*). O'Neill also tried out expressionism, an artistic movement that strove to depict the world not with the objectivity of realism, but in a more subjective way, colored by characters' perceptions and the events of the play. Expressionism merely suggested an outside world, stripping down drama to a few settings and characters, sketching the outside world, using iconic types for characters, and compressing dialogue to the essentials. O'Neill's use of these techniques led critics to label his *Emperor Jones* the first American expressionist play.

O'Neill continued to develop themes he had explored in earlier plays. The expressionistic play *The Hairy Ape* continued his investigation of the search for identity. *Desire Under the*

Elms used a more naturalistic tone to examine the psychological underpinnings of a family in disarray, while still relying heavily on symbolism and monologues. *The Great God Brown* investigated the conflict of idealism and materialism using poetry and masks.

In the latter part of O'Neill's writing career, he rejected pure expressionism and the most highly theatrical of his previous devices, returning to naturalism while retaining a subtler form of symbolism. During this period, he produced his most celebrated and fully developed work. In particular, he honed his skills at depicting realistic, psychological close-ups of his characters. Mining his unhappy childhood for themes and characters, he wrote his most autobiographical plays: *Long Day's Journey into Night*, *The Iceman Cometh*, and *Moon for The Misbegotten*. These plays are notable for their length and repetition of themes and ideas.

These plays show O'Neill bringing together his previous themes in powerful and haunting ways. *Long Day's Journey into Night*, generally regarded as his best play, brings together several lost souls in the same family. As in previous plays, these characters' pipe dreams are the only way they can sustain themselves in a hostile world. The mother is a drug addict, the father is a failed actor who has spent his life compromising his ideals in favor of gratifying the audience's tastes, the older son is a bitter alcoholic, and the younger son is a disillusioned invalid. Over the course of one day, the members of the family lose their pipe dreams and struggle to find some sense of purpose in their lives. It is in these later plays, and especially *Long Day's Journey into Night*, that O'Neill finally found the dramatic form that expressed his inner vision.

Question

Complete the chart below to summarize information about Eugene O'Neill's writing career. Match each statement with the phase of O'Neill's career that it best describes. This question is worth 3 points.

1st Phase	• _____
	• _____
2nd Phase	• _____
	• _____
3rd Phase	• _____

Answer Choices (Choose 5 to complete the chart.)

(A) He won several Pulitzer Prizes.

(B) He began experimenting with symbolism.

(C) He wrote plays based on his own life.

(D) He wrote emotional, action-filled plays.

(E) His own life as an actor affected his writing.

(F) He began to look to European writers as his role models.

(G) He became more interested in showing subjective viewpoints than in realism.

2.

Sand Painting in Two Cultures

Navajos in the American Southwest and Australian Aboriginals lived on different continents with no hint of contact prior to modern times, and yet both cultures developed the art of creating designs on the ground with sand and other colored substances found in nature. Both indigenous peoples have traditionally used sand painting in religious rituals. While both traditions are unique to their particular environment and culture, both traditions create impermanent visual art that is incorporated with music, dance, and storytelling in the context of belief systems in which life is not divided between religious and secular activities. While the term "sand painting" is often used to describe both traditions, "ground art" is the term commonly used in Australia.

Aboriginal art is rooted in "Dreamtime", the time when ancestor spirits dreamed the earth and its inhabitants into being. Dreamtime, unlike ordinary chronological time, exists simultaneously in the past, present, and future. Aboriginal clans in Australia employ ritual activities to access Dreamtime and the power found in specific places. Ground art, songs, and dance enact and bring into present-day experience the ancestral spirits who created the local animals, plants, and rock formations, as well as events in the clan's past, such as successful hunts and the discovery of water sources.

When a nomadic Australian aboriginal clan comes to a new site, they gather for a ground art ritual. Clan members create designs with different colored sand, feathers, plants, stones, and other objects. Many of the designs are essentially "maps", with symbols referring to specific features of the local landscape and also events that occurred there in Dreamtime. These rituals are normally secret: the songs, dances, and designs have power and are intended only for clan members. Through reenacting the creation myths and clan history associated with the given area, cultural beliefs as well as knowledge useful for survival are passed from one generation to the next. When the ritual is completed, the painting is scattered.

While traditional Navajos have very different gods and belief structures from those held by Australian aboriginal clans, they too have no separation between religious and secular worlds. Navajos also have ancestral beings or gods ("the Holy People") that were active in creating specific local natural features. In addition, Navajos also believe that the sacred beings are active and involved in the daily life of the people.

The Navajos (who also refer to themselves as Diné) use sand painting in extensive rituals called "sings". Sings are ceremonies that involve many relatives and friends and are intended to bless, protect, or heal the individual for whom they are held. Sand painting plays a central role in the ceremony, but singing and dancing are also included. A design specific to the particular ritual is painted with sand, charcoal, pollen, and clay on the ground inside the hogan. The images portray mountains and other features of the region, the gods who created them, and legends and stories from the past. The sand painting is considered a living being: when the "patient" lies on the image, the power of the gods is absorbed, and harmony is restored within his or her life. When the ritual is completed, the sand and other elements are returned to the earth.

In both these traditional cultures, visual art is created on the ground for ritual use; both cultures consider the artwork to have life and power; both cultures integrate the visual art with dance and song and stories; and both cultures destroy the images at the end of the ceremonies. Contrasting with cultures rooted in Western Europe, religion in these cultures is not separate from daily life, visual art is not separate from other arts, such as music and dance, and art is not a commodity created for consumers.

Both of these cultures, however, have been influenced by western European cultures. In modern times, individual artists in both cultures have adapted traditional designs for permanent art to be sold to outsiders. Navajo weavers now incorporate sand painting designs into their blankets, and other Navajo artists create permanent sand paintings by gluing the colored sand onto various backings. Most Navajo artists alter the design somewhat to avoid a curse from the "Holy People" for depicting sacred designs outside of prescribed rituals. Modern-day Australian aboriginal artists also use designs that resemble their traditional ground art in paintings made with sand or with paint. Like Navajo artists, they alter the prescribed ritual designs, keeping the exact ritualistic patterns secret to their clan.

Question

Complete the chart below to summarize information about sand painting in Australian Aboriginal and Navajo cultures. Match each statement with the culture with which it is associated. This question is worth 3 points.

Australian Aboriginals	• _____ • _____
Navajos	• _____ • _____ • _____

Answer Choices (Choose 5 to complete the chart.)

(A) Use sand painting as part of rituals meant to connect clan members with the gods and with the past.

(B) No longer participate in rituals involving sand paintings, except as reenactments for tourists.

(C) Incorporate clay, charcoal, and pollen into their painting designs.

(D) Preserve the paintings for a certain amount of time after completing the ritual.

(E) Make use of feathers, plants, and stones as well as sand to create their painting designs.

(F) Use modified sand painting designs in blankets, which are made to be sold to tourists.

(G) Use sand painting designs as a central part of healing rituals.

Skills Practice

Read the following passages and choose the best answer. The paragraphs are numbered for you.

Inductive and Deductive Reasoning

1 Galileo rolled balls down inclined planes, measuring the distances and times the balls traveled until he noticed patterns, and then decided that everything falls at the same speed. Albert Einstein daydreamed, thinking about the rules that govern bodies and motion, and wondered what would happen if a person sat on a beam of light. Both were great scientists, and they thought in two different ways.

2 Galileo used *deductive reasoning*, that is, he collected data until he recognized a pattern, and then he came up with a law of nature to describe his observations. We have come to think that this is the most important way to do science. However, other great scientists, such as Einstein, have used the other logical method, *inductive reasoning*. Inductive reasoning starts with the grand laws, the big picture, and then applies the laws to individual situations. Deductive reasoning moves from the specific to the general; inductive reasoning moves from the general to the specific. Great minds have used both methods in benefit of scientific research.

3 In the late 1600s, Robert Hooke was an experimentalist who used deductive reasoning. He hung weights from springs of different materials and masses to see how far the springs could stretch before they could no longer rebound. Similarly, he measured the resistance of springs by compressing them with weights and found that the more a spring was compressed, the greater its resistance to the force. These are examples of deductive reasoning. The results of Hooke's experiments have made mattresses more comfortable, staplers work reliably, and pogo sticks bounce higher.

4 Einstein knew the laws of physics that Isaac Newton, James Maxwell, and other great thinkers had already formulated. According to Maxwell's theories, the energy of electrons emitted from a surface should change according to the brightness of the light shown upon them. Like other scientists at the turn of the twentieth century, Einstein was confounded by the discovery of a scientist named Heinrich Hertz: The energy of electrons emitted from a surface did not vary according to the intensity of the light shown upon them, but according to the color. Using bits and pieces of other scientists' work, Einstein determined that light must travel as little bundles of energy, called photons, and that the energy of the photons depended on the color of the light. This is an example of inductive reasoning because Einstein applied the known laws of nature to a specific question. Einstein's idea revolutionized scientific understanding. After several years of controversy, he was eventually awarded the Nobel Prize for this discovery in 1921. During those years of controversy, Einstein's detractors had argued against his receiving the prize because Einstein neither ran experiments in a laboratory nor used deductive reasoning to arrive at his conclusions.

5 Deductive reasoning has indeed led to some faulty conclusions at times. For instance, in the medieval period in Europe, which was a particularly unproductive time for science, a "gentleman scientist" observed this phenomenon: When peasants became overheated

while working, they would often throw their wool shirts off into the hay in the barn and forget about them. After a few weeks, mice would emerge from under the wool shirt. Thus, he deduced that wool shirts and hay created mice, a misconception that continued for centuries.

6 Inductive reasoning has also led to mistakes. The first scientists, who lived in Greece in the fourth century B.C., were called natural philosophers. They prized inductive reasoning and observation. They reasoned that since the circle was the most perfect shape, then everything in the heavens had to be spherical or circular. ■ (**A**) That meant all the planets had to be spheres, and their orbits had to be circular. As further study made scientists' observations better and more precise, the orbits began to appear elliptical, as we now know them to be. ■ (**B**) But the Greek natural philosophers would not surrender their idea of perfection. ■ (**C**) They depicted circular orbits whose centers were on the circumference of the original orbit to explain the new shapes. As the scientists who inherited this tradition made more precise observations, they added more circles generated from other circles, until there were thousands of them. ■ (**D**)

Passage 1

1. Which of the following can be inferred from paragraph 2 about deductive reasoning?
   (A) It is often considered superior to inductive reasoning.
   (B) It cannot adequately explain certain laws of nature.
   (C) It is not generally used by modern scientists.
   (D) It is more logical than inductive reasoning.

2. According to paragraph 3, what did Robert Hooke want to learn through his experiments with springs?
   (A) How to make springs out of different materials
   (B) How much different kinds of springs weigh
   (C) How springs act in different conditions
   (D) How to make a better spring mattress

3. According to paragraph 4, what was confusing about Hertz's discovery?
   (A) It contradicted previously accepted theories.
   (B) It was the result of deductive, not inductive, reasoning.
   (C) It disproved a discovery made by Einstein.
   (D) It could not account for the varying brightness of light.

4. According to paragraph 4, which of the following is true about Einstein's work?
   (A) He worked very closely with both Maxwell and Hertz.
   (B) He attempted to disprove a theory about electrons and light.
   (C) He made a discovery that contradicted Newton's laws of physics.
   (D) He used inductive reasoning to make a discovery that won him a prize.

5. The word controversy in paragraph 4 is closest in meaning to
   (A) conversation
   (B) delay
   (C) disagreement
   (D) effort

6. The word which in paragraph 5 refers to
   (A) Europe
   (B) conclusion
   (C) medieval period
   (D) deductive reasoning

7. The word phenomenon in paragraph 5 is closest in meaning to
   (A) ritual
   (B) report
   (C) practice
   (D) occurrence

8. What can be inferred about the scientist discussed in paragraph 5?
   (A) He did numerous experiments with mice.
   (B) His conclusions about mice were widely accepted.
   (C) His scientific methods were copied throughout Europe.
   (D) He was concerned about working conditions for peasants.

9. The word precise in paragraph 6 is closest in meaning to
   (A) numerous
   (B) accurate
   (C) difficult
   (D) varied

10. Look at the four squares [■] in paragraph 6 that indicate where the following sentence could be added.

    With the invention of the telescope, after almost 2,000 years of belief in circular orbits, scientists were finally forced to admit that planetary orbits were elliptical.

    Where would the sentence best fit?

11. Why does the author discuss the natural philosophers' views on planetary orbits in paragraph 6?
    (A) To give an example of inductive reasoning
    (B) To illustrate the development of inductive reasoning
    (C) To show that inductive reasoning is not always accurate
    (D) To explain why deductive is better than inductive reasoning.

12. Complete the chart below to summarize information about deductive and inductive reasoning. Match each phrase with the method it describes. This question is worth 3 points.

Deductive Reasoning	• ____ • ____ • ____
Inductive Reasoning	• ____ • ____

Answer Choices (Choose 5 to complete the chart.)

(A) Was initially developed by Galileo

(B) Looks for patterns in a collection of facts

(C) Was used to understand the behavior of springs

(D) Applies general laws to specific situations

(E) Was the only method used by Einstein

(F) Does not necessarily rely on laboratory experiments

(G) Was inaccurately used to describe the origin of mice

Passage 2

The Presidency of John Tyler

1 John Tyler, the tenth president of the United States, is not one of the nation's better-known presidents. In fact, it may be from the campaign slogan, "Tippecanoe and Tyler too", that people remember his name, though not the man himself—a man who never actually ran for the presidency, but became president by default.

2 It was Tyler's running mate, William Henry Harrison, the "Tippecanoe" in the 1840 slogan, who was elected president. The catchy but somewhat obscure slogan derives from the Tippecanoe River in Indiana, the site of a battle which Harrison fought against Native Americans. Just 32 days after his inauguration Harrison died from pneumonia, leaving the position of the presidency open to his vice president, Tyler. The circumstances of Tyler's presidential ascendancy led to his unfortunate nickname, "the accidental president", a moniker many historians say overshadows his presidential successes. Furthermore, many historians see Tyler's perceived obscurity as mistaken, taking pains to point out his positive place in American presidential history. Scholarly works on Tyler point out that while his term, from 1841 to 1845, may have been riddled with fruitless clashes between the parties (the Whigs, formerly the National Republicans and Tyler's party at the time he took office) and the Democrats (a.k.a. the Jacksonians), his tenure also boasts presidential victories and historic firsts.

3 First and foremost, Tyler was the first vice president to become president because of the death of his predecessor. This was not an insignificant event. ■ (**A**) There was no precedent for Tyler's claim to the White House and no clear, undisputed process laid out in the U.S. Constitution. ■ (**B**) Tyler, however, asserted that the Constitution gave him the power to run the country, and he had himself sworn into office soon after Harrison's death. ■ (**C**) More than one hundred years later, Tyler's ability to produce a fairly quick and orderly transfer of power became the model for the 25th Amendment to the U.S. Constitution, ratified in 1967. ■ (**D**)

4 There were other successes, too. Tyler was president at a time in the country's history when many families from the East were moving West to start new lives on unsettled lands. The "Log Cabin" bill was enacted during Tyler's administration and enabled these settlers to claim unsettled land before it was offered for public sale. Through the bill, settlers were granted sections of acreage and the opportunity to pay for the land later. In addition, in 1842 Tyler signed a tariff bill protecting Northern manufacturers. His legacy also includes the Webster-Ashburton treaty that ended a Canadian boundary dispute and the 1845 annexation of Texas, which significantly increased not only the size of the country, but its importance in the hemisphere. Despite these historic and precedent-setting successes, Tyler vanished into presidential obscurity after leaving office.

5 Tyler, who was born to an old Virginia ruling-class family a few years after the American Revolution, was part of the Old Virginia aristocracy in the White House, which had included such illustrious presidents as Washington and Jefferson. As a wealthy Southern planter with extensive land holdings, Tyler opposed a strong army, tariffs, and extending the vote to men without property. He also held fast and steady to the Southern

notion of slavery, a concept that inevitably led to his downfall. In actuality, Tyler's belief that slavery was part of the young nation's destiny was a great contradiction for the Virginian, who believed in the liberties and freedoms that were integral to the Constitution. Though Tyler is believed to have understood the evils of slavery, he defended the institution until his death, contributing, many believe, to what ultimately became the Civil War.

6 By 1845, the man who graduated from the College of William and Mary at the age of seventeen, studied law, served in the House of Representatives, and served as Governor of Virginia, had had enough of the presidency. He moved back to Virginia with his second wife (he was the first president to get married while in office), Julia Gardiner Tyler. When the first Southern states seceded from the nation in 1861, Tyler chaired the Richmond Convention, which attempted to reconcile the North and South. When then-president Lincoln rejected Tyler's proposed compromises, Tyler became a leading proponent of Southern secession. The secession of the Southern states from the rest of the country quickly led to the Civil War.

1. According to paragraph 2, all of the following are true about John Tyler EXCEPT that:
   (A) He was elected president 32 days after Harrison left office.
   (B) He was a member of the Whig political party.
   (C) He was vice president under Harrison.
   (D) He served as president for four years.

2. Which of the following sentences best expresses the information in the highlighted sentence in paragraph 2?
   (A) The nickname accidentally given to Tyler foretold his success as president.
   (B) The unfortunate nickname given to Tyler kept him from achieving success as president.
   (C) Tyler's unflattering nickname became more widely known than his achievements as president.
   (D) Although Tyler became president under unfortunate circumstances, he went on the achieve great success.

3. The phrase taking pains in paragraph 2 is closest in meaning to
   (A) risking opposition
   (B) suffering hardship
   (C) making efforts
   (D) feeling sorry

4. Which of the following can be inferred from paragraph 2 about Tyler's presidency?
   (A) Political conflicts overshadowed Tyler's successes.
   (B) Historians generally consider Tyler to be insignificant.
   (C) Tyler did not achieve much while he was president.
   (D) Tyler could never have won a presidential election.

5. According to paragraph 3, what happened in 1967?
   (A) A president died during his term in office.
   (B) An addition was made to the U.S. Constitution.
   (C) A bill originally designed by Tyler was finally passed.
   (D) Tyler was finally acknowledged for an important success.

6. Look at the four squares [■] in paragraph 3 that indicate where the following sentence could be added.

   It clearly states, "In case of the removal of the President from office or of his death or resignation, the Vice President shall become President."

   Where would the sentence best fit?

7. The author's description of Tyler's achievements in paragraph 4 mentions which of the following?
   (A) Designs for log cabins
   (B) A peace treaty with Texas
   (C) A journey to Canada
   (D) Land grants for settlers

8. The word dispute in paragraph 4 is closest in meaning to
   (A) disagreement
   (B) requirement
   (C) extension
   (D) limitation

9. The word integral in paragraph 5 is closest in meaning to
   (A) added
   (B) basic
   (C) potential
   (D) allowed

10. The author's summary of Tyler's adult life in paragraph 6 mentions which of the following?
    (A) His first wife's name
    (B) The law firm where he first worked
    (C) The college where he got his diploma
    (D) His length of service in the House of Representatives

11. **According to the information in paragraph 6, what did Tyler do after leaving the office of the presidency?**

    (A) He got married for the second time.

    (B) He moved away from Virginia permanently.

    (C) He became a soldier and fought in the Civil War.

    (D) He led efforts to prevent a war between the North and South.

12. **The word proponent in paragraph 6 is closest in meaning to**

    (A) designer

    (B) supporter

    (C) financer

    (D) enemy

13. **An introductory sentence for a brief summary of the passage is given below. Complete the summary by choosing THREE answers that best represent the main ideas in the passage. This question is worth 2 points.**

    Although John Tyler is a relatively unknown president, he did important things while in office.

    -
    -
    -

Answer Choices

    (A) Tyler was the first person to rise from vice president to president following the death of his predecessor in office.

    (B) While Tyler was in office, there were frequent clashes between the Whig and Democrat political parties.

    (C) The 25th Amendment to the U.S. Constitution, ratified in 1967, was modeled on Tyler's ascendance to the presidency.

    (D) Although Tyler passed important bills that supported the country's expansion into new territories, this did not bring him lasting fame.

    (E) Because of his Southern background, Tyler supported slavery even though it was in contradiction to his other beliefs, and this eventually led to his downfall.

    (F) Tyler was active in attempts to reconcile North and South in the period leading up to the Civil War.

Passage 3

American Poet: Emily Dickinson

1   The name Emily Dickinson (1830–1886) often evokes images of a shy, solitary woman, dressed in white, writing poetry, hiding away from the outside world in her prominent family's Amherst, Massachusetts home. Such perceptions of a life of seclusion, however, fail to appreciate the originality, non-conformity, and sheer audacity of Dickinson's deservedly famous verse. Dickinson may have lived a safe and quiet life tucked away in her family home, but there is nothing safe about her poetry. In fact the bold vision of her poetry—and the public reaction which it likely would have caused—may be the reason that Dickinson shut herself away and did not seek to publish her poems.

2   Dickinson's poetry departed radically from standard poetic form. At a time when poems were fairly formal and predictably structured, Dickinson's were fluid and seemingly structureless. One of her contemporaries called her poetry "spasmodic" and "uncontrolled". Recent critics, however, have pointed out that many of her poems are structured like stanzas in a hymn or ballad and that much of her poetry emulates the kind of meter found in hymns. Dickinson's poetry, therefore, is hardly random in its form. It simply does not adhere to the standard poetic forms of her day. At the same time, despite their hymn-like qualities, Dickinson's works also violated many rules of hymn meter. Many of her poems, for example, fail to follow a standard rhyme pattern and break off a line where no natural pause would exist in speech or song.

3   Dickinson also experimented with punctuation. She used dashes liberally, placing them where colons, commas, semicolons, and periods would normally go. The lack of periods, in particular, gives a deliberately unfinished and transient quality to her verse. Periods close an idea, but dashes convey a conscious refusal to create endings, as seen in her poems. Thus, rather than randomly placing dashes, as early critics suggested, Dickinson used them to reinforce her poetic themes. The placement of dashes reinforces the musicality of her poetry, indicating where the verse slows its pace and where it speeds up. In fact, the dashes in her original manuscripts are not uniform: they are long, short, and sometimes vertical, as in musical notation. Some of the dashes in her original handwritten manuscripts seem to curve upward or downward, leading some scholars to speculate that the markings were intended to indicate the emphasis of certain words or phrases.

4   Dickinson's use of capitalization was similarly experimental. Throughout her poetry, she capitalized words in seemingly random ways. The editors who published her work immediately after her death revised and standardized her capitalization so that only the first word of a line was capitalized. However, later scholars have restored her original capitalization, believing that Dickinson intended the capitals to emphasize important words or concepts. In other places, the capitals signal metrically stressed words. As demonstrated in her stanza form and her punctuation, Dickinson created her own unconventional rules for poetry. Yet, she did not simply defy traditional norms randomly; rather, she used such poetic elements to reinforce her themes.

5 The themes explored in Dickinson's poetry are as unconventional as her poetic structure. Indeed, critics observe that she needed to develop her own kind of poetry in order to truly express her own boldly innovative ideas. Originally, scholars saw her poetry as sentimental and religious, but more recent examinations have revealed how daring her views of life truly were. The hymn-like qualities of her verses suggest a religious sensibility, and her work shows a deep spirituality, but she saw this spirituality as accessible through private experience that was inseparable from the daily routines and mundane details of life. She marveled at the myriad aspects of the natural world, which she valued for its own sake. Her poetry shows that she rejected traditional ideas because she felt that prevailing societal norms could not allow her to be true to herself. Therefore, retreat from society and introspection were her only routes to understand life and the spiritual aspects of being. Dickinson's poetry reveals a woman who was not quiet and shy despite her seclusion, but one who questioned and often rejected many fundamental beliefs of her contemporaries and the society around her.

1. Why does the author begin the article by describing the common image of Dickinson as a "shy recluse"?
   (A) To explain why Dickinson's poetry is so unusual
   (B) To describe what Dickinson's daily life was like
   (C) To help the reader understand Dickinson's personality
   (D) To contrast it with the author's own view of Dickinson

2. According to paragraph 1, which of the following is true of Dickinson?
   (A) She was a constant seeker of publicity.
   (B) She was deeply unhappy that her work was not published.
   (C) She may have feared that her poems would not be well-received.
   (D) She probably thought her work did not deserve the attention it got.

3. Which of the following sentences best expresses the information in the highlighted sentence in paragraph 2?
   (A) Dickinson has been criticized for imitating well-known ballads and hymns.
   (B) Dickinson based many of her poems on the popular hymns and ballads of her day.
   (C) Many of Dickinson's poems have a structure and rhythm similar to that of hymns and ballads.
   (D) In addition to her poetry, Dickinson has also been praised for her many hymns and ballads.

4. The word violated in paragraph 2 is closest in meaning to
   (A) broke
   (B) listed
   (C) created
   (D) followed

5. The word deliberately in paragraph 3 is closest in meaning to

   (A) hopefully

   (B) pleasantly

   (C) innocently

   (D) purposely

6. According to paragraph 3, which of the following is true about Dickinson's writing?

   (A) She often placed periods, commas, and colons incorrectly.

   (B) She emphasized certain words and phrases by underlining.

   (C) She made frequent use of different types of dashes.

   (D) She included musical notes in her poems.

7. The word them in paragraph 3 refers to

   (A) periods

   (B) dashes

   (C) endings

   (D) ideas

8. According to paragraph 4, Dickinson used capital letters in certain ways to show

   (A) how much she disliked the rules of punctuation

   (B) which ideas in a poem were more important

   (C) where each new line or stanza should begin

   (D) which parts of a poem she planned to revise

9. The word metrically in paragraph 4 is closest in meaning to

   (A) rhythmically

   (B) consistently

   (C) strongly

   (D) lightly

10. Which of the following can be inferred from paragraph 5 about Dickinson's habits?

   (A) She spent time observing nature.

   (B) She frequently attended church.

   (C) She read many sentimental books.

   (D) She was bored by her daily routines.

11. The phrase marveled at in paragraph 5 is closest in meaning to

   (A) was interested in

   (B) was amazed by

   (C) looked closely at

   (D) spoke about

12. **In paragraph 5, the author describes Dickinson as**

    (A) timid and quiet

    (B) traditionally religious

    (C) sentimental and shallow

    (D) original and introspective

13. **An introductory sentence for a brief summary of the passage is given below. Complete the summary by choosing THREE answers that best represent the main ideas in the passage. This question is worth 2 points.**

    Emily Dickinson was an unconventional poet.

-
-
-

Answer Choices

    (A) Dickinson was a shy woman who lived a quiet, reclusive life.

    (B) The structure of Dickinson's poetry does not follow the norms of her day.

    (C) Dickinson used punctuation in unusual ways.

    (D) Dickinson's work was edited to follow standard rules of capitalization.

    (E) The expectations of society made it difficult for Dickinson to be true to herself.

    (F) Dickinson used poetry to express her unique understanding of spirituality.

READING PRACTICE TEST

Read the following passages and answer the questions. You may take notes.

Passage 1

The Building of the Transcontinental Railroad

1 The Transcontinental Railroad, which connected the East Coast and Midwestern regions of the United States with California on the West Coast, is considered one of the greatest technological achievements in U.S. history. It made such an impact on the U.S. economy that its construction has been compared to the development of the atomic bomb, the digging of the Panama Canal, and the landing of man on the moon. In fact, the success of the two-thousand-mile-long railroad built over harsh desert terrain and through mountains of granite was much more than economic. Its effects were far reaching and touched every aspect of American life.

2 Travel across the continent saw an immediate and dramatic transformation. Prior to the railroad, there were two basic ways to get across the great frontier: by horse-pulled stagecoach or wagon, or by boat. Travel by stagecoach could cost upwards of $1,000, took five or six months, and involved crossing over treacherous mountains and barren deserts. Travel by sea meant an eighteen-thousand-mile ocean voyage around the tip of South America and north up the Pacific Coast. There was a shortcut of sorts that included a land crossing through the rugged Isthmus of Panama and then a northern traverse of the Pacific by ship to California. But even this trip took months, was filled with risks, such as disease, and was still expensive. With the construction of the transcontinental railroad, the trip across the continent could be completed in a miraculous five days for a cost of just $150 for first-class accommodations.

3 The rail project began in 1863 while the Civil War was raging in the eastern part of the country. The Central Pacific Railroad began building the railroad east from Sacramento, California while the Union Pacific Railroad began building west from Omaha, Nebraska. Although shifts were kept working around the clock, the pace through the mountains was excruciatingly slow, moving forward at an average of only about a foot a day. Work crews blasted tunnels through the Sierra Nevada Mountains by hand, drilling holes in rock and packing the holes with explosive powder.

4 Thousands of Chinese, Irish, and German immigrants, as well as former Union and Confederate soldiers and freed slaves contributed to the six-year-long job of constructing the railroad. The two work teams, Union Pacific and Central Pacific, finally met up on May 10, 1869 at Promontory Summit, in Utah, where the final "golden spike" was ceremoniously driven into the railroad bed.

5 The effect of the railroad was profound and far-reaching, even finding its way into the American vocabulary. Phrases such as "time's up", "time's a wasting", and "the train is leaving the station", became part of the vernacular. The railroad unified the nation, but ironically led to its division into four standard time zones. At the same time, construction of the railroad resulted in the creation of hundreds of new towns in an area that had once been called "the Great American Desert" because it was considered unsuitable for

cultivation, and therefore, uninhabitable by people dependent upon agriculture for subsistence. This area east of the Rocky Mountains, including the mid-western territories of North and South Dakota, Nebraska, Kansas, and Oklahoma, as well as part of Texas and New Mexico, was a flat wasteland, devoid of trees and bone-dry. Add in Colorado, Wyoming and Montana, and the "new frontier" was viewed as a major obstacle to America's expansion; that is, until the construction of the railroad. With the Transcontinental Railroad, the Great American Desert fast became America's breadbasket, a major agricultural region of the country. Soon, too, it was discovered that this former wasteland was home to many of the country's richest mines. Settlers rushed in, leading the 1890 census to declare that the American frontier had disappeared.

6   The railroad led to changes on the East Coast, as well. Western agricultural products, coal, and minerals traveled west to east, changing the way the nation ate, built, and conducted business. There was a moral impact, too. Completion of the railroad fostered a new American faith that, with money and determination, the people of the United States could accomplish anything.

1. How does the author compare the Transcontinental Railroad to the Panama Canal in paragraph 1?

    (A) They both cost a great deal of money to build.

    (B) They are of equal importance in U.S. history.

    (C) They each took a long time to build.

    (D) They are similar in length.

2. The word its in paragraph 1 refers to

    (A) the Transcontinental Railroad

    (B) the Panama Canal

    (C) the atomic bomb

    (D) the U.S. economy

3. The word treacherous in paragraph 2 is closest in meaning to

    (A) tall

    (B) rocky

    (C) numerous

    (D) dangerous

4. According to paragraph 2, all of the following are true about cross-continental travel prior to the building of the railroad EXCEPT:

    (A) It took about half a year to cross the country by stagecoach.

    (B) A first-class stagecoach ticket could cost as much as $150.

    (C) The trip by sea could be shortened by going overland across Panama.

    (D) The journey around South America was about eighteen thousand miles.

5. According to paragraph 3, which of the following is true about the construction of the Transcontinental Railroad?

   (A) It was slowed down by inexperienced workers.
   (B) It started in California and ended in Nebraska.
   (C) It went on for twenty-four hours a day.
   (D) It was delayed by the Civil War.

6. Why does the author describe how workers blasted tunnels through the mountains in paragraph 3?

   (A) To give an example of how difficult it was to build the railroad
   (B) To compare the working conditions of the two different teams
   (C) To explain work methods that were common at the time
   (D) To show how skilled the railroad workers were

7. According to paragraph 4, which of the following is true about the Transcontinental Railroad?

   (A) Its two teams began working together in Utah.
   (B) It was half completed when it reached Utah.
   (C) Its two sections were joined in Utah.
   (D) It only went as far as Utah.

8. The word spike in paragraph 4 is closest in meaning to

   (A) coach
   (B) board
   (C) train
   (D) nail

9. The word vernacular in paragraph 5 is closest in meaning to

   (A) dictionary
   (B) language
   (C) workday
   (D) business

10. What can be inferred from paragraph 5 about the area east of the Rocky Mountains prior to the construction of the railroad?

    (A) It was considered unsuitable for farming.
    (B) New towns were constantly being built in the region.
    (C) There were no human inhabitants in that region.
    (D) It was covered with an abundance of trees.

11. According to paragraph 6, what effect did the railroad have on life in the eastern United States?

    (A) The prices of coal and minerals rose in the East.

    (B) More people in the East started working in agriculture.

    (C) Eastern business failed because of competition from the West.

    (D) Western products became more available to East Coast residents.

12. The word faith in paragraph 6 is closest in meaning to

    (A) rule

    (B) wish

    (C) belief

    (D) religion

13. An introductory sentence for a brief summary of the passage is given below. Complete the summary by choosing THREE answers that best represent the main ideas in the passage. This question is worth 2 points.

    The Transcontinental Railroad had profound effects on American life.

    -
    -
    -

Answer Choices

(A) Travel across the country had been time-consuming, risky, and expensive, but the railroad changed all that.

(B) Immigrants from several countries, as well as former soldiers and former slaves, were among those who helped build the railroad.

(C) Work crews labored hard to build the railroad, completing it in just six years.

(D) The United States is large enough to require division into four different time zones.

(E) The completion of the railroad facilitated the settlement of the mid-western United States and its transformation into an important agricultural area.

(F) The Transcontinental Railroad improved access to some of the country's richest mines in previously unsettled areas.

Passage 2

Ardi: Our Ancient Ancestor

1   Over a century ago, Charles Darwin hypothesized that human beings, *Homo sapiens sapiens*, and the great apes had evolved from a common ancestor. ■ (**A**) By seeking fossil remains, scientists hoped to chronicle hominid species that existed in the six million years before *Homo sapiens sapiens*. ■ (**B**) One of the many problems in searching for fossilized skeletons is that only under ideal conditions can bones last millions of years, and the likelihood of finding a complete, or nearly complete, skeleton is very small. ■ (**C**) In the 1920s and 1930s, in Zhaukudian, China, what people called "dragon bones" were identified as fossilized remains of *Homo erectus*, the Peking Man, from about 400,000 years ago. Those remains were of the first species known at that time to have migrated from Africa. ■ (**D**) In 1974, in Ethiopia, Donald Johanson discovered the remains of a 3.2 million-year-old hominid, whom they named Lucy, an *Australopithicus* hominid. In 1984 in Kenya, Kamoya Kimeu discovered the Turkana Boy, an *Australopithecus* boy from about 1.6 million years ago. It was clear from these fossil remains that *Homo sapiens sapiens* had gone through more than one evolutionary step between its chimpanzee-like ancestor and the present species.

2   In 1992, in Ethiopia, Gen Suwa of the University of Tokyo found a single upper molar from a species that predated Lucy. Later, other scientists found skeletal bones in this same area. Tim White of the University of California at Berkeley, led the team that spent the ensuing 15 years digging up, cataloging, and studying bones until they had a nearly complete skeleton. This skeleton took many more years to analyze than other skeletons because it was crushed by something extremely heavy before it was fossilized. Using sophisticated instruments and techniques, Dr. White's team reconstructed the original shape of the bones. Their years of painstaking work has resulted in Ardi, which is short for the name of the new species, *Ardipithecus ramidus*. She, for she is a she, is about 4.4 million years old, 1.2 million years older than Lucy. Ardi is now the oldest known ancestor of *Homo sapiens sapiens*.

3   Ardi is about four feet tall, about a foot taller than Lucy, and she weighed about 120 pounds. From the pelvic bones, it appears that she walked upright but still retained her tree-climbing abilities—the feet are not arched, and the big toe is prehensile. Her hands are more like those of the great apes, and she has long arms and short legs. Ardi's skull held a chimpanzee-sized brain. Her canine teeth, as well as male canine teeth also found, are not the outsized canines used in ritual mating displays in primates, but are the same size as the other teeth. The molars show that Ardi was an omnivore and did not depend on a diet largely of fruits as do present-day chimpanzees.

4   All the plant and animal fossils around Ardi's and other *Ardipithecus* bones were excavated, so scientists have been able to analyze the environment in which Ardi lived. Because humans walk upright, scientists had surmised that humans and great apes diverged when hominids left the forests to live on the grassy savannahs, where bipedalism would be an advantage. However, the plant and animal remnants collected and analyzed show that Ardi lived in a cool, woodland habitat. The area is now a hot, arid desert, making it a good area for preserving the bones.

5 In addition to Ardi's skeleton, Professor White's team discovered bones from 36 other individuals, all belonging to *Ardipithecus ramidis*. In Chad and Kenya, other teams have discovered skeletal remains from the same period as *Ardipithecus*, but of different hominid species. Some scientists speculate that more than one kind of hominid was alive at the same time, thus causing some to wonder if Lucy or Ardi or both are not direct ancestors of humans, but off-shoots from our common line. This diversity of hominid species has also led to the radical speculation that *Homo sapiens sapiens* may have evolved from more than one kind of hominid. Humans may not have one common ancestor after all.

1. According to paragraph 1, what was discovered in China in the 1920s and 1930s?
   (A) A very small skeleton
   (B) The bones of ancient dragons
   (C) Fossilized remains of a human ancestor
   (D) The common ancestor of apes and humans

2. Look at the four squares [■] in paragraph 1 that indicate where the following sentence could be added.

   Since then, scientists have pursued what has been called colloquially "the missing link", the earlier hominid that was halfway between the common ancestor and human beings.

   Where would the sentence best fit?

3. The word predated in paragraph 2 is closest in meaning to
   (A) hunted
   (B) was related
   (C) outlasted
   (D) came before

4. According to paragraph 2, why did it take so many years to put together Ardi's skeleton?
   (A) The bones were extremely old.
   (B) Dr. White's team was very small.
   (C) The instruments were not sophisticated.
   (D) The skeleton had been severely damaged.

5. The word prehensile in paragraph 3 is closest in meaning to
   (A) unusually large
   (B) near the front
   (C) able to grasp
   (D) extra long

6. According to paragraph 3, all of the following are true about Ardi EXCEPT:

   (A) She weighed less than Lucy.

   (B) She could climb trees.

   (C) She had flat feet.

   (D) She had ape-like hands.

7. According to paragraph 3, which of the following is true about Ardi's teeth?

   (A) They were used in ritual mating displays.

   (B) They are similar to a chimpanzee's teeth.

   (C) They show that she ate a varied diet.

   (D) They vary greatly in size.

8. The word surmised in paragraph 4 is closest in meaning to

   (A) concluded

   (B) discovered

   (C) realized

   (D) taught

9. Which of the following can be inferred from paragraph 4 about early hominids?

   (A) They were forced out of their forest habitat by the great apes.

   (B) They started walking upright while still living in forests.

   (C) They died out because their forest habitat became desert.

   (D) They eventually left the forest because the environment was too cool.

10. According to paragraph 5, what did Dr. White's team find besides Ardi's skeleton?

    (A) Proof that humans have more than one common ancestor

    (B) Remains of others members of the same species as Ardi

    (C) Bones belonging to other hominid species

    (D) Evidence of the ancestors of great apes

11. Which of the following sentences best expresses the information in the highlighted sentence in paragraph 5?

    (A) Since Lucy and Ardi are from the same ancestral line as humans, scientists no longer have to speculate about the common ancestor of humans and apes.

    (B) Since several species of hominid may have existed during the same period, scientists wonder whether Ardi and Lucy are actually ancestors of human beings.

    (C) Scientists speculate that the different hominid species recently discovered were direct ancestors of both Lucy and Ardi.

    (D) Scientists can only guess about the ancestral lines of Lucy, Ardi, and other hominid species.

12. The word radical in paragraph 5 is closest in meaning to

   (A) accepted

   (B) logical

   (C) extreme

   (D) influential

13. An introductory sentence for a brief summary of the passage is given below. Complete the summary by choosing THREE answers that best represent the main ideas in the passage. This question is worth 2 points.

   The discovery of the hominid species *Ardipithecus ramidus* (also called "Ardi") may shed new light on our understanding of the evolution of human beings.

   -
   -
   -

Answer Choices

   (A) One difficulty that scientists have had is that it is very unusual to find fossilized skeletons that have lasted for millions of years.

   (B) Previously, the oldest known hominid remains were those of Lucy, a 3.2-million-year-old hominid discovered in 1974.

   (C) The bones of an *Australopithecus* boy, known as "Turkana Boy", were discovered in Kenya several years before the first discovery of bones belonging to Ardi.

   (D) The fact that Ardi's skeleton had been crushed before fossilization made it particularly challenging to analyze.

   (E) Like humans, Ardi walked upright and was an omnivore, but she also had characteristics similar to chimpanzees.

   (F) The fact that Ardi lived in a woodland environment changed the previous idea that the evolution of apes and humans diverged when our hominid ancestors left the forest for life on the plains.

Passage 3

Two Intriguing New Planets

1 Recent discoveries of two planets in outer space have raised new questions and possibilities in the study of astronomy. In August 2009, researchers in the United Kingdom, led by Andrew Collier Cameron of the University of St. Andrews, Scotland, discovered a new planet, named WASP-17b, that, contrary to all other known planets within or outside of our solar system, rotates in the opposite direction from its star. The group United Kingdom's Wide Area Search for Planets (WASP) worked with Switzerland's Geneva Observatory. WASP-17b is the largest and the dense extra-solar planet (that is, a planet outside the solar system) discovered thus far. It is almost twice the size of Jupiter, but has less than fifteen percent of Jupiter's mass. Located approximately one thousand light years away, WASP-17b, is also the closest known planet to its star.

2 In our solar system, all planets orbit the sun in the same direction as the sun itself is turning. Most scientists believe this is because the sun and planets all evolved out of one original mix of gases and dust particles. There had been an expectation that extra-solar planets would follow the same pattern. The planets in our solar system also follow an orbit that has the shape of a disc. Over 370 exoplanets (another name for extra-solar planets) have been discovered since 1995, and only three of these do not follow the familiar pattern of a disc-shaped orbit. In each of these three cases, the planet rotates around its star in the same direction as the star's rotation, but with an axis that is tilted somewhat.

3 WASP-17b was discovered using the transit method: that is, measuring the dimming of the light from its star as the planet passes between the star and the observers. ■ (**A**) Further calibrations determined the unusual backward rotation. ■ (**B**) Coel Hellier, of Keele University, believes a larger planet also rotating around the star may have altered WASP-17b's rotational direction by passing close by. ■ (**C**) He believes that a near-collision with the right trajectory acted like a gravitational slingshot that flung one of the planets into a retrograde orbit. ■ (**D**)

4 Another team member, Andrew Collier Cameron of the University of St. Andrews, believes it is more likely that WASP-17b has an as-yet-undetected neighboring body whose gravity causes the planet to gradually change its orbit over time. He theorizes that WASP-17b once orbited its star in the same direction as the star's rotation, but that its rotation gradually tilted away from the axis of the star's rotation until it was perpendicular and continued tilting until it reached its current reverse rotation. If Cameron's theory is correct, eventually WASP-17b will once again be rotating in the same direction as the star.

5 In addition to the transit method used to discover WASP-17b, astronomers use many other ways to discover new planets. Most of the discoveries to date have used the radial velocity method, which measures the wobble of a star caused by the gravitational pull of a planet. The Hubble Space Telescope has played an important role in this method.

6 In May of 2009, Stuart Shaklan and Steven Prado, astronomers at the United States National Aeronautics and Space Administration's (NASA) Jet Propulsion Laboratory, announced that they had discovered a new planet using astrometry, a method of searching for planets that was first tried fifty years ago, but which had not previously been successful. Shaklan and Prado measured the motions of thirty stars over a period of twelve years, looking for variations in each star's location caused by the gravitational pull of a planet. The planet they found, VB 10b, is a gas giant approximately twenty light-years away, with six times the mass of Jupiter, and it orbits a star that is the smallest star known to be orbited by a planet. Prado feels that strometry is optimal for discovering other solar system configurations like our own, that might hold other Earths. As new techniques and instruments have been developed, the rate of discovery of new planets has increased every year, along with exponential growth of data, leading to new understandings and new theories about planet formation and the birth of the universe.

1. The word particles in paragraph 2 is closest in meaning to
   (A) clouds
   (B) pieces
   (C) areas
   (D) storms

2. According to paragraph 2, what did scientists expect to be true about extra-solar planets?
   (A) They would have a tilted axis.
   (B) They would not follow a disc-shaped orbit.
   (C) They would have evolved out of gas and dust.
   (D) They would rotate in the same direction as their stars.

3. According to paragraph 3, how is the transit method used to detect the presence of a planet?
   (A) It measures how the star's light changes when it is blocked by the planet.
   (B) It measures how long it takes for light from the star to reach observers.
   (C) It measures the strength of the star's light when it reaches the planet.
   (D) It measures how much light from the star is reflected by the planet.

4. The word calibrations in paragraph 3 is closest in meaning to
   (A) observations
   (B) measurements
   (C) instruments
   (D) researchers

5. Look at the four squares [■] in paragraph 3 that indicate where the following sentence could be added.

Team members are not in agreement about a probable cause.

Where would the sentence best fit?

6. The word whose in paragraph 4 refers to
    (A) the orbit
    (B) WASP-17b
    (C) a neighboring body
    (D) Andrew Collier Cameron

7. According to paragraph 4, what does Andrew Collier Cameron believe is the likely cause of WASP-17b's unusual rotational direction?
    (A) The speed at which the planet travels
    (B) The shape of the planet's orbit
    (C) A nearby object in space
    (D) Gravity from its star

8. Why does the author discuss different methods used to discover planets in paragraph 5?
    (A) To highlight the importance of the discovery of VB 10b by astrometry
    (B) To increase the reader's confidence in the work of astronomers
    (C) To introduce information about the Hubble Space Telescope
    (D) To explain how WASP-17b was discovered

9. According to paragraph 5, which of the following is true about the Hubble Space Telescope?
    (A) It played an important role in the discovery of WASP-17b.
    (B) It has not been particularly useful in the discovery of new planets.
    (C) Its measurements are more accurate than those of other instruments.
    (D) It has been used to search for new planets by the radial velocity method.

10. The word wobble in paragraph 5 is closest in meaning to
    (A) speed
    (B) route
    (C) shaking
    (D) heaviness

11. The word optimal in paragraph 6 is closest in meaning to
    (A) unreliable
    (B) useful
    (C) accurate
    (D) best

12. **Which of the following sentences best expresses the information in the highlighted sentence in paragraph 6?**

(A) Technological developments have increased the discovery of new planets, and these discoveries have increased our understanding of how the universe was formed.

(B) As new technologies are developed, we will discover more planets and collect more data about the universe.

(C) Every year, new instruments and new technologies are developed, based on theories that have been proposed about the formation of planets and of the universe.

(D) The discovery of new planets will contribute to the development of new techniques and instruments for exploring the universe and collecting data.

13. **An introductory sentence for a brief summary of the passage is given below. Complete the summary by choosing THREE answers that best represent the main ideas in the passage. This question is worth 2 points.**

The recent finding of two extra-solar planets contributes to the development of our research and understanding of outer space.

-
-
-

Answer Choices

(A) The planet WASP-17b is the only known planet to rotate in a direction opposite of its star's rotation.

(B) Although WASP-17b is a great deal larger than Jupiter, it is also less dense, and it is the largest known extra-solar planet.

(C) Most extra-solar planets, like the planets in our solar system, have an orbit that is in the shape of a disc.

(D) There are several theories, but no agreement, about the reason for the unusual rotational direction of WASP-17b.

(E) Most extra-solar planets have been discovered with the use of a method known as "radial velocity".

(F) Different methods have been used to discover planets, and the discovery of the planet VB 10b was the first successful use of the astrometry method.

Facts About Listening

Skills

Basic Comprehension

Skill 1   Main Ideas
Skill 2   Purpose
Skill 3   Detail

Pragmatic Understanding

Skill 4   Function
Skill 5   Attitude

Connecting Information

Skill 6   Organization
Skill 7   Relationships
Skill 8   Inferences

Skills Practice

Listening Practice Test

In the Listening section of the TOEFL iBT™, you will listen to six passages and respond to five or six questions about each passage. The Listening section includes 4–5 minute lectures and 2–3 minute conversations. All of the conversations are about academic topics.

The chart on page 112 shows you how the lectures and conversations compare. It also shows scoring and what the questions measure. Pages 113–115 show you examples of what the screens look like for Listening.

Most questions in Listening are multiple-choice with one answer. Some questions require you to refer to a photo or drawing, and some questions require more than one answer. These include chart questions, which are worth more than one point.

The whole Listening section takes 60–90 minutes. You will hear each of the passages only one time. You should take notes about key points as you listen to the passages.

Facts About Listening

Academic Lecture	4–6 academic lectures with one or more speakers
Content	Arts, Life Science, Physical Science, Social Science
Length	Approximately 500–800 words per lecture
Time	3–5 minutes per lecture
Questions	6 questions per lecture
Total Time	60–90 minutes

Campus Conversation	2–3 conversations
Content	Office counseling, arranging services
Length	Approximately 12–25 exchanges per conversation
Time	3 minutes per conversation
Questions	5 questions per conversation
Total Time	60–90 minutes

Score	0–30

Question formats	Multiple-choice with single answer
	Multiple-choice with two answers
	Sequence
	Matching

Question types	Main idea
	Purpose
	Detail
	Function
	Attitude
	Organization
	Relationships
	Inferences

Measures ability to	Understand main idea
	Recognize a speaker's attitude
	Recognize a speaker's degree of certainty
	Understand purpose
	Understand relationships
	Make inferences
	Recognize organization
	Recognize topic changes

Sample Listening Screens

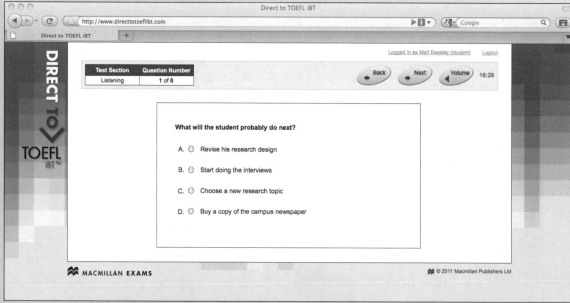

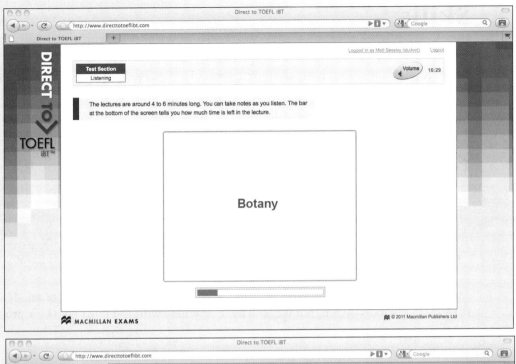

The lectures are around 4 to 6 minutes long. You can take notes as you listen. The bar at the bottom of the screen tells you how much time is left in the lecture.

Botany

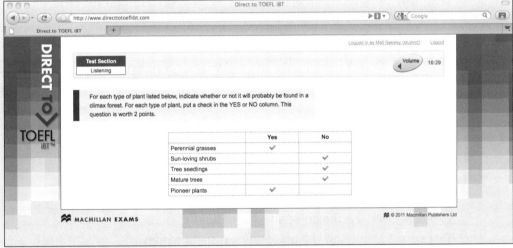

For each type of plant listed below, indicate whether or not it will probably be found in a climax forest. For each type of plant, put a check in the YES or NO column. This question is worth 2 points.

	Yes	No
Perennial grasses	✓	
Sun-loving shrubs		✓
Tree seedlings		✓
Mature trees		✓
Pioneer plants	✓	

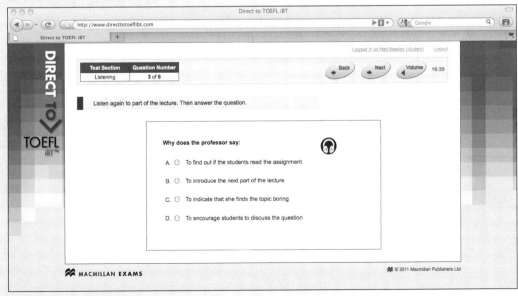

Test Section	Question Number
Listening	3 of 6

Listen again to part of the lecture. Then answer the question.

Why does the professor say:

A. ◯ To find out if the students read the assignment

B. ◯ To introduce the next part of the lecture

C. ◯ To indicate that she finds the topic boring

D. ◯ To encourage students to discuss the question

Skills

Basic Comprehension

Some questions test your basic comprehension of a passage by asking you about main ideas and details, or about the speaker's purpose.

Skill 1   Main Ideas

A main idea question asks you for the general idea or the main topic of the lecture or conversation.

Examples

What is the main topic of the lecture?

What is the conversation mainly about?

What aspect of the [*subject*] does the speaker lecture about?

What is bothering the speaker?

As you listen to the lecture or conversation, take notes. Each time you hear an idea, make a note. If the idea is discussed again, put a check by it. The idea with the most checks is probably the main idea.

Practice

Listen to these parts of conversations and lectures. Take notes. Then answer the questions.

Tip	Always read the questions for each section before you listen. This will help guide your listening.

1. **What is the topic of the student's research project?**

(A) Types of opinion polls

(B) Student who have scholarships

(C) People who use the university gymnasium

(D) Feelings about how the university has spent money

2. **What is this conversation mainly about?**

(A) The college work-study program

(B) The best ways to study

(C) The student's professional goals

(D) Problems facing new students

3. **What is this conversation mainly about?**

(A) Courses offered by the Psychology Department

(B) Prerequisites for Educational Psychology

(C) The student's spring semester schedule

(D) A difficult class assignment

4. What is this lecture mainly about?

  (A) The field trip schedule

  (B) Old field succession

  (C) Natural disasters

  (D) Local plant species

5. What is this lecture mainly about?

  (A) Victorian Literature

  (B) A novel by Elizabeth Gaskell

  (C) The Industrial Revolution

  (D) Poverty in Victorian England

6. What is this lecture mainly about?

  (A) How toys help babies learn

  (B) Experiments done with babies

  (C) Abstract thinking skills in children

  (D) A theory of cognitive development

Skill 2   Purpose

A *purpose question* asks you for the reason a conversation or lecture is taking place. Purpose questions are more common in conversations than lectures. Purpose questions often begin with *Why*.

Examples

  Why does the student need to see the housing officer?

  Why did the professor ask to see the student?

  Why does the lecturer talk about the auto industry?

  What is the main purpose of the lecture?

As you listen to the lecture or conversation, listen for a particular problem. In a conversation, the student is usually the one who has a problem. What is it?

Practice

Listen to these parts of conversations and lectures. Take notes. Then answer the questions.

1. Why does the student visit the professor?

  (A) To get the professor's approval for his research project

  (B) To find out the professor's opinion about the new gym

  (C) To get help in applying for a scholarship

  (D) To discuss his background reading

2. **Why is the student talking to the counselor?**

    (A) To get some career advice

    (B) To find out how to get a work-study job

    (C) To get information about the bookstore

    (D) To discuss changing her major

3. **Why is the student talking to the advisor?**

    (A) To get help choosing a major

    (B) To plan his research project

    (C) To work out his course schedule

    (D) To find out which classes are required

4. **What is the main purpose of the lecture?**

    (A) To give background knowledge for the field trip

    (B) To prepare students for an upcoming exam

    (C) To explain the professor's grading system

    (D) To introduce a game

5. **What is the main purpose of the lecture?**

    (A) To help students choose a novel to read

    (B) To outline the topics for the semester

    (C) To prepare students for reading a novel

    (D) To give the rationale for class assignments

6. **What is the main purpose of the lecture?**

    (A) To describe the midterm exam

    (B) To outline the rest of the semester

    (C) To explain an important concept

    (D) To review previously taught material

Skill 3   Detail

A *detail question* asks you to identify specific facts that support or provide information on a subject.

Examples

What does the student need to show to the advisor?

According to the professor, why did Lafayette help the Americans?

What is an example of parasitism?

Some detail questions ask you to choose two answers. Both of the answers must be correct for you to get the point. As you listen to the lecture or conversation, take notes and include specific facts and details about the topic. Sometimes the speaker will talk about several things; keep notes on all the details on all the topics.

Practice

Listen to these parts of conversations and lectures. Take notes. Then answer the questions.

1. **What information will the student look for in the campus newspaper?**
   - (A) The amount of money it cost to build the new gym
   - (B) How much money each issue of the newspaper costs
   - (C) Different ideas for spending the money that was used for the gym
   - (D) The names of people who gave the university money for the new project

2. **Where has the student worked in the past?**
   - (A) At a high school
   - (B) At a daycare center
   - (C) At a bookstore
   - (D) At a college

3. **Why is the student having difficulty with his schedule?**
   - (A) The class that he really wants to take is full.
   - (B) None of his required courses are on the spring schedule.
   - (C) He changed his major from Psychology to Education.
   - (D) Two courses that he wants to take are scheduled at the same time.

4. **According to the lecture, what kinds of plants move in to take the place of the pioneer plants?**

   Choose 2 answers.

   - A Young trees
   - B Smaller shrubs
   - C Annual plants
   - D Perennial grasses

5. **What is one thing novelists Dickens and Gaskell hoped to do with their writing?**
   - (A) Increase awareness of bad working-class conditions in their country
   - (B) Portray the problems faced by the middle and upper classes
   - (C) Improve on the work of novelists such as Thackeray and Trollope
   - (D) Make novels the predominant literary form of the era

6. **What is "object permanence"?**
   - (A) An ability to reach for objects
   - (B) A type of toy suitable for young infants
   - (C) A way of teaching babies how to use objects
   - (D) A step in the development of thinking skills

Pragmatic Understanding

Some questions test your understanding of things NOT directly stated in the conversation or lecture. This is referred to as *pragmatic understanding*.

Skill 4   Function

A *function question*, like an inference question, asks you to come to conclusions based on what you hear. For example, a student may say to a friend, "We've been studying all morning, and it's lunchtime". The speaker wants to stop studying and have lunch. Instead of directly saying, "Let's stop and have lunch". the speaker implies, indirectly suggests, this by mentioning how long they have been studying and that it is lunchtime.

For this type of question, you will often hear the relevant part of the conversation or lecture again.

Examples

What is the student trying to get from his professor?

What does the student imply when she says this: (*audio replay*)

Why does the counselor say this: (*audio replay*)

The answer choices will not match exactly the words in the conversations or lectures. You will have to determine the function.

 Practice

Listen to these parts of conversations and lectures. Take notes. Then answer the questions.

1. **Listen again to part of the conversation. Then answer the question.**

   Why does the professor say this:
   (A) To discourage the student from spending too much money on the project
   (B) To suggest that the student improve his research design
   (C) To encourage the student to keep the research simple
   (D) To remind the student to keep track of his expenses

2. **Listen again to part of the conversation. Then answer the question.**

   What does the counselor mean when he says:
   (A) The student should wait a minute while he attends to something else.
   (B) The student should not count on getting the job she hopes for.
   (C) The student will probably be hired for the position she wants.
   (D) The student might not be able to find employment this semester.

3. **Listen again to part of the conversation. Then answer the question.**

   Why does the student say this:
   (A) He wishes the class started later in the day.
   (B) He wants to know the reason for the schedule.
   (C) He prefers morning to afternoon classes.
   (D) He wonders why early classes are required.

DIRECT TO TOEFL iBT™

4. **Listen again to part of the lecture. Then answer the question.**

   Why does the professor ask:

   (A) He wants to give an example of an exam question.

   (B) He wants a student to provide the answer.

   (C) He wants to introduce the topic of the lecture.

   (D) He wants students to discuss the question.

5. **Listen again to part of the lecture. Then answer the question.**

   Why does the professor say:

   (A) To announce that the class will watch a movie about Gaskell

   (B) To indicate uncertainty about her opinion of Gaskell's novels

   (C) To refer to the fact that the class will read one of Gaskell's novels

   (D) To mention the date that Gaskell's work will be discussed in class

6. **Listen again to part of the lecture. Then answer the question.**

   Why does the student say:

   (A) To correct her mistaken answer

   (B) To ask for time to find the answer

   (C) To give someone else a chance to answer

   (D) To imply that she doesn't know the answer

Skill 5 Attitude

An *attitude question* asks for information NOT directly stated in the conversation or lecture. Like *Function* in Skill 4, this information can be inferred from the whole conversation. A speaker may be unhappy or happy; anxious or amused. She or he may dislike or like something. The speakers will not directly express their feelings, but will still let you know how they feel.

Examples

What is the student's attitude about working in groups?

How does the professor feel about late papers?

What does the student mean when she says this: (*audio replay*)

A speaker's tone of voice, the length of the sentences, and the adjectives and adverbs used will all provide clues to a speaker's attitude.

> **Tip**   As you listen, think about how you might feel in a similar situation.

Practice

Listen to these parts of conversations and lectures. Take notes. Then answer the questions.

1. How does the student feel about the professor's suggestion to look at newspapers?
   (A) It might be a problem.
   (B) He does not want to spend the money.
   (C) He does not mind doing it.
   (D) It would take a lot of time.

2. How does the student feel about working in the college bookstore?
   (A) She wants to because she has had similar experience.
   (B) She would prefer to get a different kind of job.
   (C) She is afraid it would not be easy.
   (D) She thinks it would be an educational experience.

3. How does the student feel about the Research Methods class?
   (A) He is looking forward to taking it.
   (B) It should be a fascinating class.
   (C) He thinks he might like it.
   (D) He does not really want to take it.

4. How does the professor feel about field trips?
   (A) They are not very much fun.
   (B) They are a valuable part of the course.
   (C) They are sometimes a mistake.
   (D) They are not of much importance.

5. What is the professor's opinion of Gaskell's novel, *Wives and Daughters*?

(A) It is not well done.

(B) It is uninteresting.

(C) It is too complicated.

(D) It is her finest work.

6. What is the professor's opinion of Renée Baillargeon's experiment about object permanence?

(A) It was a very good idea.

(B) It did not prove anything of interest.

(C) There are too many arguments against it.

(D) Its value has been underrated.

Connecting Information

Some questions test your understanding of how things in the passage are related. These relationships may be either stated or implied.

Skill 6 Organization

An *organization question* asks how the conversation or lecture is organized. The information in a passage may be organized in many ways, including chronologically from early to later, steps from start to finish or from easiest to more difficult, concept and definition, similarities and differences, or main idea and example.

Examples

> Why does the professor discuss erosion?
>
> How does the professor introduce global warming?
>
> What point does the professor make when she mentions consumer spending?

An organization question will more likely follow a lecture than a conversation. Listen carefully to examples presented in the lecture and try to determine why they are used.

Practice

Listen to these parts of conversations and lectures. Take notes. Then answer the questions.

1. Why does the professor discuss ecological succession?
   - (A) To give an example of the process of old field succession
   - (B) To compare that process to the process of old field succession
   - (C) To define a broader category that includes old field succession
   - (D) To give an example of something that is not old field succession

2. Why does the professor mention Romanticism?
   - (A) To identify it as the style of the novel the class will read
   - (B) To explain who influenced Gaskell as a writer
   - (C) To criticize its approach to writing
   - (D) To compare it with Victorian literature

3. Why does the professor bring up the stages of cognitive development as defined by Jean Piaget?
   - (A) To review material previously discussed
   - (B) To introduce a topic that will be on the exam
   - (C) To finish the discussion on cognitive development
   - (D) To explain the meaning of the term "cognitive development"

4. **What point does the professor make when he describes Renée Baillargeon's experiment?**

   (A) Piaget inspired many other researchers.

   (B) Piaget's ideas may not have been entirely correct.

   (C) Piaget was better at designing experiments.

   (D) Piaget was considered to be the father of cognitive development.

Skill 7 Relationships

A relationship question asks how ideas are related. You might be asked to summarize the information in a different way from the lecture. Many of these questions are in the form of charts.

Examples

How are these modes of transportation compared?

What classifications could fit these types of manufacturing?

Why does the professor mention the Civil War?

Label the process in this diagram.

Tip	When you see a chart among the questions, you should take notes that resemble the categories and style in the chart.

Practice

Listen to these parts of conversations and lectures. Take notes. Then answer the questions.

1. **Who will the student interview for his research project? For each type of person, put a check in the correct column. This question is worth 2 points.**

	Interview	Not Interview
Students		
Trustees		
University president		
Faculty		
Staff		

2. **Why is the student looking for a job?**

   (A) It is required for her major.

   (B) She wants to have the work experience.

   (C) The counselor has recommended it.

   (D) She needs to earn some money.

3. Which of the following classes will the student probably take in the spring?

(A) Research Methods and Statistics

(B) Child Development and Statistics

(C) Educational Psychology and Research Methods

(D) Child Development and Educational Psychology

4. For each type of plant listed below, indicate whether or not it will probably be found in a climax forest. For each type of plant, put a check in the YES or NO column. This question is worth 2 points.

	YES	NO
Perennial grasses		
Sun-loving shrubs		
Tree seedlings		
Mature trees		
Pioneer plants		

5. Based on information given in the lecture, indicate whether the statements below describe Elizabeth Gaskell as a writer. For each statement, put a check in the YES or NO column. This question is worth 2 points.

	YES	NO
She wrote about working and living conditions among the lower classes.		
She focused largely on the middle and upper classes.		
She only wrote novels.		
She was interested in beauty and nature.		
She wanted to portray life realistically.		

6. Based on information given in the lecture, indicate whether each statement below describes Jean Piaget or Renée Baillargeon. For each item, put a check in the correct column. This question is worth 2 points.

	Jean Piaget	Renée Baillargeon
Described four stages of cognitive development		
Believed that object permanence develops around 4 months of age		
Believed that object permanence develops around 9 months of age		
Did an experiment using toys hidden behind a curtain		
Did an experiment using objects moving across a screen		

Skill 8 Inferences

An *inference question* asks for information that is NOT directly stated. You will have to make a judgment based on the entire passage.

Examples

What does the student imply when she says this: (*audio replay*)

What can be inferred about the concert?

What will the student probably do next?

Since the answer is implied, the answer choices will not match exactly the vocabulary used in the conversation or lecture.

Practice

 Listen to these parts of conversations and lectures. Take notes. Then answer the questions.

1. What will the student probably do next?
   (A) Revise his research design
   (B) Start doing the interviews
   (C) Choose a new research topic
   (D) Buy a copy of the campus newspaper

2. What will the student probably do next?
   (A) Have a meal at the cafeteria
   (B) Visit the daycare center for a job interview
   (C) Get help writing a résumé
   (D) Ask some people to write letters of reference

3. What will the student probably do?

   (A) Sign up for a summer class
   (B) Quit his job at the library
   (C) Register for spring classes tomorrow
   (D) Take some time to think about his schedule

4. What does the professor imply about animal life in the early stages of old field succession?

   (A) It is not very diverse.
   (B) It consists mainly of insects.
   (C) It does not change much.
   (D) It is not very attractive.

5. What will the class probably do after reading Elizabeth Gaskill's novel?

   (A) Read something from the Romantic period
   (B) Read a biography of Charlotte Brontë
   (C) Read a twentieth-century English novel
   (D) Read a novel by another Victorian author

6. What will the professor probably discuss in the next class session?

   (A) More about object permanence
   (B) Other experiments done by Piaget
   (C) The work of Renée Baillargeon
   (D) Other theories of cognitive development

🎧 Skills Practice

Listen to the following lectures and conversations, and answer the questions.

Lecture 1

1. What is this lecture mainly about?
   - (A) A unique ecosystem
   - (B) Natural habitats of Siberia
   - (C) Freshwater animal species
   - (D) The effect of pollution

2. Which of these characteristics contribute to the uniqueness and diversity of plant and animal species in Lake Baikal? For each characteristic, put a check in the YES or NO column. This question is worth 2 points.

	YES	NO
The lake's crescent shape		
The age of the lake		
The isolation of the lake		
The condition of the lake's water		
The length of the lake		

3. Listen again to part of the lecture. Then answer the question.

   Why does the professor say:
   - (A) To find out if the students read the assignment
   - (B) To introduce the next part of the lecture
   - (C) To indicate that she finds the topic boring
   - (D) To encourage students to discuss the question

4. Why does the professor discuss the nerpa?
   - (A) It is the smallest seal in the world.
   - (B) It is the world's only freshwater seal.
   - (C) It is the only predator of the golomyanka.
   - (D) It is an example of an animal found only in Lake Baikal.

5. According to the lecture, what have been two sources of pollution in Lake Baikal?

Choose 2 answers.

A Construction of villages
B Pulp factories
C Logging activity
D Transportation systems

6. What will the professor probably talk about during the next lecture?

(A) Different species inhabiting other lakes
(B) The history of the logging industry around Lake Baikal
(C) Measures taken to control pollution on Lake Baikal
(D) The effect of pollution on the nerpa and the golomyanka

Lecture 2

1. What is this lecture mainly about?

(A) The continental shelf
(B) The largest islands in the world
(C) How islands form
(D) What happens when sea levels rise

2. Why does the professor mention Greenland, Madagascar, and Great Britain?

(A) To help define what an island is
(B) To give examples of continental islands
(C) To compare them to other islands
(D) To show how large islands can be

3. What is Newfoundland in Canada an example of?

(A) A peninsula
(B) A barrier island
(C) A continental island
(D) A volcano

4. Listen again to part of the lecture. Then answer the question.

What does the professor mean when he says: 🎧

(A) He will repeat what the student said.
(B) The student's answer was correct.
(C) Knowing the answer is required.
(D) He knows the student bought the textbook.

5. How does the professor feel about the reading assignment?

    (A) It is very difficult.

    (B) It is not necessary.

    (C) It is not very long.

    (D) It is easy to understand.

6. Where do volcanic islands form?

    (A) On the continental shelf

    (B) Over hotspots

    (C) Near sand deposits

    (D) In shallow waters

Lecture 3

1. What is the main purpose of the lecture?

    (A) To introduce a book the class will read

    (B) To prepare students for an assignment

    (C) To explain how to write a memoir

    (D) To generate a reading list

2. Listen again to part of the lecture. Then answer the question.

    What does the professor mean when she says:

    (A) She wants the students to feel free to ask questions.

    (B) The student should have done the homework assignment.

    (C) The student brought up the topic she was planning to discuss.

    (D) She is happy that the student is participating in the discussion.

3. How does the professor explain what memoir is?

    (A) She lists authors who have written memoirs.

    (B) She gives examples of books that are memoirs.

    (C) She compares memoir to autobiography.

    (D) She asks the students to write their memoirs.

4. **Which of the sentences describe autobiography only, which describe memoir only, and which describe both autobiography and memoir? For each statement, put a check in the correct column. This question is worth 2 points.**

	Autobiography	Memoir	Both
It is the story of the author's life.			
It focuses on facts.			
It aims to describe feelings and themes.			
It covers the author's entire life.			
It uses writing styles often found in fiction.			

5. **What does the professor imply about memoirs?**
   (A) They are more interesting to read than autobiography.
   (B) They are not usually as well-written as novels.
   (C) They tend not to be well-structured.
   (D) They contain a lot of untruths.

6. **What does the professor ask the students to bring to the next class?**
   (A) Definitions of the term "memoir"
   (B) Their personal memoirs
   (C) A list of books read
   (D) A book title

Lecture 4

1. **What is this lecture mainly about?**
   (A) The disadvantages of monoculture
   (B) Agriculture among the Iroquois
   (C) Healthy agricultural practices
   (D) Iroquois cooking traditions

2. **Listen again to part of the lecture. Then answer the question.**

   Why does the professor say:
   (A) To emphasize an important piece of information
   (B) To point out something that will be on the exam
   (C) To refer to the reading that the students did
   (D) To introduce a new topic for discussion

3. Why did Iroquois men NOT live in the village year-round?

(A) They left to hunt animals.

(B) They left to gather nuts and berries.

(C) They left to find places to grow crops.

(D) They left to hide from the Europeans.

4. Why do corn, beans, and squash grow well together?

(A) They are plants that require little growing space.

(B) They each provide something the others need.

(C) They all need the same sun and soil conditions.

(D) They are all native to the same part of the world.

5. What is the professor's opinion of Iroquois farming practices?

(A) They were better in some ways than modern farming practices.

(B) They were improved by the arrival of the Europeans.

(C) They left the crops vulnerable to disease.

(D) They required too much labor.

6. What does the professor imply about corn, beans, and squash?

(A) They improved the taste of meat and fish.

(B) They were the only foods that the Iroquois ate.

(C) They were no longer eaten after the Europeans arrived.

(D) They were the major source of nutrition for the Iroquois.

Conversation 1

1. Why is the student talking with the librarian?

(A) She can't find a book.

(B) She needs to choose a book.

(C) She wants to check out a journal.

(D) She is looking for the reference section.

2. What mistake did the student make?

(A) She used the wrong sources for her research.

(B) She misunderstood the professor's assignment.

(C) She tried to check out a book without an I.D. card.

(D) She looked for something in the wrong part of the library.

3. Where can the student find the book for her assignment?

(A) In the Economics section

(B) Near the magazines

(C) On the first floor

(D) By the librarian's desk

4. Listen again to part of the conversation. Then answer the question.

Why does the student say:

(A) To excuse herself because she's ready to leave

(B) To express regret for bothering the librarian

(C) To indicate that she doesn't understand

(D) To apologize for her mistake

5. Which of these materials can be checked out of the library and which cannot be checked out? For each item, put a check in the YES or NO column. This question is worth 2 points.

	YES	NO
Reference books		
Reserve books		
Back issues of journals		
Current issues of magazines		
DVDs		

Conversation 2

1. Why is the student talking with the professor?

(A) He needs advice about looking for a job.

(B) He does not want to take a required class.

(C) He does not know what course to take.

(D) He needs help with his course work.

2. What work experience does the student have?

(A) He worked in an office.

(B) He owned a small business.

(C) He taught several business courses.

(D) He managed a marketing department.

3. How does the professor feel about the Introduction to Marketing course?

    (A) It is only a formality, but not really necessary.

    (B) It is one of the more boring courses offered.

    (C) It is only a requirement for certain students.

    (D) It is important for all business students.

4. Listen again to part of the conversation. Then answer the question.

    What does the professor mean when she says:

    (A) The student will probably learn a lot from the course.

    (B) The student already understands the course material.

    (C) The student will tolerate the course, but may be bored.

    (D) The student should get his money's worth from the course.

5. What does the professor imply about the Marketing Research course?

    (A) The student will spend a lot of time on the assignments.

    (B) The student is required to take it for his degree.

    (C) The student does not need to take it right away.

    (D) The student should take it as soon as possible.

LISTENING PRACTICE TEST

Listen to the following lectures and conversations and answer the questions. You may take notes.

Lecture 1

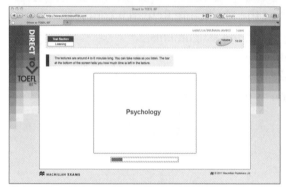

1. What is this lecture mainly about?

(A) An overview of a psychological disorder

(B) The psychological health of Americans

(C) Treatments for psychological problems

(D) The causes of psychological disorders

2. Listen again to part of the lecture. Then answer the question.

Why does the professor say this: 🎧

(A) He wants students to look the terms up in the dictionary.

(B) He wants to know who did the reading assignment.

(C) He wants a student to answer the question.

(D) He wants to introduce an explanation.

3. Why does the professor talk about the symptoms of bipolar disorder?

(A) To further define what the disorder is

(B) To explain how to diagnose the disorder

(C) To compare two different disorders

(D) To introduce treatments for the disorder

4. When does bipolar disorder usually develop?

(A) Early childhood

(B) Adolescence

(C) Early adulthood

(D) Middle or old age

5. According to the lecture, why is it difficult to diagnose bipolar disorder in children?

(A) The chemical balance in children's brains is different from that of adults.

(B) Some of the symptoms can look like normal childhood behavior.

(C) Children seldom demonstrate feelings of grandiosity.

(D) People do not expect children to have this disorder.

6. What is the professor's opinion of treatments for bipolar disorder?

(A) They last too long.

(B) They are bad for the patient.

(C) They are usually successful.

(D) They often do not work.

Lecture 2

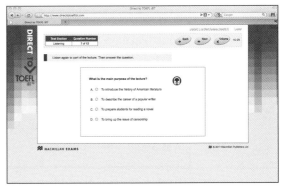

7. What is the main purpose of the lecture?

(A) To introduce the history of American literature

(B) To describe the career of a popular writer

(C) To prepare students for reading a novel

(D) To bring up the issue of censorship

8. Listen again to part of the lecture. Then answer the question.

   What does the professor mean when she says this:
   (A) She is giving the class information about a future assignment.
   (B) She will look up some information for the students later.
   (C) She needs to take a break and will return right away.
   (D) She plans to talk about this topic later in the lecture.

9. Why was young Samuel Clemens apprenticed to a printer when he was only 12 years old?
   (A) He had to help support his family.
   (B) It was the customary age to start work.
   (C) He had completed his schooling.
   (D) His family realized he had the talent for it.

10. Which story or book first brought Mark Twain fame?
    (A) *Life on the Mississippi*
    (B) *Jim Smiley and His Jumping Frog*
    (C) *The Adventures of Tom Sawyer*
    (D) *The Adventures of Huckleberry Finn*

11. Based on information given in the lecture, indicate whether each statement below describes *The Adventures of Tom Sawyer, The Adventures of Huckleberry Finn,* or both books. For each statement, put a check in the correct column. This question is worth 2 points.

	The Adventures of Tom Sawyer	The Adventures of Huckleberry Finn	Both books
Took place on the Mississippi River			
Had characters based on people from Twain's hometown			
Was about small town life			
Dealt with slavery and freedom			
Caused a lot of controversy			

12. **How did Mark Twain react to the censorship of his book?**

   (A) He thought it was a bad thing.

   (B) He predicted it would sell more books.

   (C) He considered rewriting the first 100 pages.

   (D) He made public statements against censorship.

Lecture 3

13. **What is this lecture mainly about?**

   (A) Daily life among the Aztecs

   (B) Aztec gods and religion

   (C) The Spanish conquest of the Aztecs

   (D) A valuable food in Aztec culture

14. **Listen again to part of the lecture. Then answer the question.**

   What does the professor mean when he says this: 🎧

   (A) He wants to make sure he forgets nothing.

   (B) He wants to introduce the next topic.

   (C) He wants to review material already discussed.

   (D) He wants to finish the lecture early.

15. **Why does the lecturer tell about the myth of the origin of the cacao tree?**

    (A) To give an example of an Aztec god

    (B) To help explain the Aztec belief system

    (C) To show how highly the Aztecs valued chocolate

    (D) To give a background to the history of Spanish explorers

16. **Who was Quetzalcoatl?**

    (A) A god

    (B) A priest

    (C) An explorer

    (D) An emperor

17. **According to the lecture, how did the Aztecs use cacao beans?**

    Choose 2 answers.

    [A] As decorations for their cloaks

    [B] As a tribute from conquered people

    [C] As a beverage reserved for nobility

    [D] As a fertilizer for their cornfields

18. **How does the professor feel about the chocolate drink prepared by the Aztecs?**

    (A) It was not spicy enough.

    (B) It must have tasted good.

    (C) It was normally too sweet.

    (D) It sounds unpleasant to drink.

Lecture 4

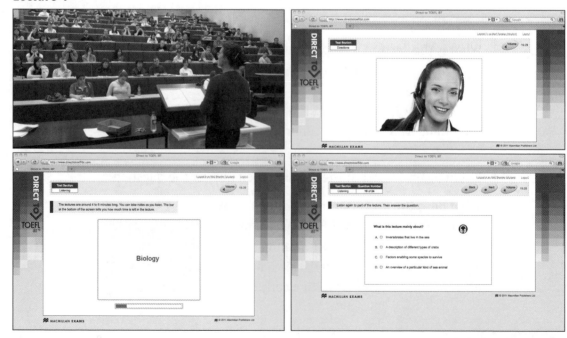

19. **What is this lecture mainly about?**

    (A) Invertebrates that live in the sea
    (B) A description of different types of crabs
    (C) Factors enabling some species to survive
    (D) An overview of a particular kind of sea animal

20. **Listen again to part of the lecture. Then answer the question.**

    Why does the professor say:

    (A) To bring up a previous reading assignment
    (B) To refer to something she mentioned earlier
    (C) To remind students of a previous discussion
    (D) To imply that she wants no more interruptions

21. **How does a horseshoe crab's shell look?**

    (A) Bumpy
    (B) Smooth
    (C) Soft
    (D) Sharp

22. **What do horseshoe crabs eat?**

    (A) Barnacles
    (B) Flatworms
    (C) Clams and worms
    (D) Scorpions and spiders

23. **According to the lecturer, indicate which of the characteristics listed below contributed to the survival of the horseshoe crab for 300 million years. For each characteristic, put a check in the YES or NO column. This question is worth 2 points.**

	YES	NO
Its hard shell		
Its special body shape		
Its method of molting		
Its ability to go for a year without eating		
Its tolerance of temperature changes		

24. **In what type of climate did horseshoe crabs first thrive?**
    (A) Temperate
    (B) Tropical
    (C) Semi-tropical
    (D) Ice age

 Conversation 1

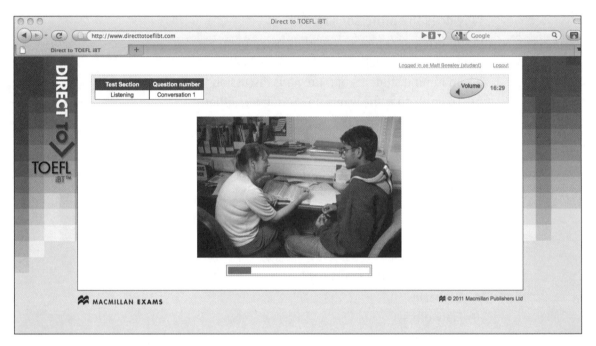

25. **What does the student need help with?**

(A) Choosing a graduate program

(B) Completing an application

(C) Finishing his undergraduate degree

(D) Finding professors to write recommendations

26. **What is the student's undergraduate major?**

(A) Chinese

(B) History

(C) Asian Studies

(D) Political Science

27. **Why should the student fill out the last page of the application?**

(A) He wants to hire a tutor.

(B) He wants a job as a tutor.

(C) He wants a position as a teaching assistant.

(D) He wants to apply for the Work-Study Program.

28 **According to the advisor, indicate which of the items below need to be included in the student's graduate school application and which do not. For each item, put a check in the YES or No column.**

	YES	NO
Test scores		
Grade transcript		
Recommendations		
Financial need statement		
Application fee		

29. **Listen again to part of the conversation. Then answer the question.**

What does the professor mean when she says:

(A) The student will probably be accepted into graduate school.

(B) The student will have a complete application.

(C) The student is ready to get his degree.

(D) The student can go home now.

🎧 Conversation 2

30. **Why is the student talking with the professor?**

   (A) She wants to be excused from some classes.
   (B) She needs help planning a project.
   (C) She has to make up missed work.
   (D) She failed the midterm exam.

31. **What will the student do one week from today?**

   (A) Take a quiz
   (B) Buy a textbook
   (C) Borrow some notes
   (D) Report on chapters 20 to 25

32. **How does the professor feel about the field trips he assigns?**

   (A) They aren't fun.
   (B) They take too much time.
   (C) They aren't as vital as other activities.
   (D) They are an important part of the course.

33. **Listen again to part of the conversation. Then answer the question.**

   What does the professor mean when he says: 🎧

   (A) The student will realize the assignment is worthwhile.
   (B) The assignment will put the student in a good mood.
   (C) The professor wants the student to be happy.
   (D) Most people enjoy visiting the museum.

34. **What subject does the professor probably teach?**

   (A) Spanish
   (B) Art History
   (C) Anthropology
   (D) Local History

Facts About Speaking

Skills

Question 1: Personal Preference

Skill 1   Description
Skill 2   Opinions
Skill 3   Specific Information

Question 2: Personal Choice

Skill 4   Compare and Contrast
Skill 5   Specific Explanations

Question 3: Campus Situation Read/Listen/Speak

Skill 6   Point of View

Question 4: Lecture Read/Listen/Speak

Skill 7   Determine the Purpose

Question 5: Campus Situation Listen/Speak

Skill 8   Problem/Solution

Question 6: Lecture Listen/Speak

Skill 9   Citing and Summarizing

General Speaking Skills

Skill 10 Word Families and Stress
Skill 11 Sentence Stress
Skill 12 Transition Words and Intonation
Skill 13 Lists and Intonation

Skills Practice

Speaking Practice Test

In the Speaking section of the TOEFL iBT™, you will respond to six questions.

The first two questions are **Independent Speaking Tasks**. For these two questions, you will give a spoken response to a question asking you for your personal preference, and a question asking you to choose between options and provide reasons for your choice. Your answers will come from your own experiences and opinions.

The other four questions in Speaking are **Integrated Speaking Tasks**. These four questions integrate reading, listening, and speaking or listening and speaking. The questions relate to campus life or academic lectures and readings. You may, for example, have to compare views, explain relationships, choose among solutions, or summarize. These are the kinds of activities you will do on campus and in your academic work.

The chart on pages 148–149 shows you how the six questions compare in content and how much time you have to prepare and speak for each question type. It also shows scoring and what the questions measure. Pages 150–153 show you examples of what the screens look like for the six question types.

The whole Speaking section takes approximately 20 minutes. You can take notes during this section. You will record your spoken responses on computer. Your responses will be sent by computer to a scoring center, where they will be rated.

Facts About Speaking

Independent Task	Speak

Question 1 — **Personal Preference**

Content — Personally important places, people, events, or activities

Question — Describe a personal preference and give reasons

Time — Preparation time: 15 seconds

Response time: 45 seconds

Question 2 — **Personal Choice**

Content — Two behaviors, alternatives, or courses of action

Question — Choose between two alternatives and defend choice

Time — Preparation time: 15 seconds

Response time: 45 seconds

Integrated Task	Read/Listen/Speak

Question 3 — **Campus Situation**

Topic — Summarize

Content — Campus-related issue

Length — 75–100 word reading passage

150–180 word listening passage (60–80 seconds)

Question — Read a notice and summarize a speaker's opinion about the content

Time — Preparation time: 30 seconds

Response time: 60 seconds

Question 4 — **Academic Course**

Topic — General/Specific

Content — Definition, process, or idea from academic subject

Length — 75–10-word reading passage

150–220-word listening passage (60–90 seconds)

Question — Combine and convey general information from the reading passage and specific information from the lecture

Time — Preparation time: 30 seconds

Response time: 60 seconds

Integrated Task	Listen/Speak
Question 5:	**Campus Situation**
Topic	Problem/Solution
Content	Student-related problem with two solutions
Length	180–220 word listening passage (60–90 seconds)
Question	Show understanding of the problem and express an opinion about the best solution
Time	Preparation time: 20 seconds
	Response time: 60 seconds
Question 6	**Academic Course**
Topic	Summarize/Explain
Content	An academic term or concept with examples
Length	230–280 word listening passage (60–90 seconds)
Question	Summarize the lecture and talk about the relationship between the examples and the overall topic
Time	Preparation time: 20 seconds
	Response time: 60 seconds

Score	0–4 for each question
	0–30 scaled score for Speaking section
Measures ability to	Complete the task
	Sustain discourse
	Speak clearly and fluently
	Use basic and complex grammar
	Use a variety of words
	Develop topic clearly with appropriate detail

Sample Speaking Screens

Question 1: Personal Preference

Question 2: Personal Choice

Sample Speaking Screens

Question 3: Campus Situation. Read/Listen/Speak

Question 4: Lecture. Read/Listen/Speak

Question 5: Campus Situation. Listen/Speak

Question 6: Lecture. Listen/Speak

Skills

Question 1   Personal Preference

Question 1 in Speaking is a personal preference question. You may be asked to describe something or give an opinion. You will be expected to give specific details to support your ideas and opinions.

Skill 1   Description

In Question 1, you may be asked to describe some activities or events, and why these activities or events are important to you. Don't just list activities. Think of something interesting to say about each one. For example, talk about how long it took, say why you liked it, give some details about what it involved, or use some adjectives to describe it.

Example

Describe some things you do at a museum you enjoy visiting.

Tip	Make sure you understand the question before you respond.

Example notes/Example response

Topic: A museum you enjoy visiting

Question: Describe some things you do at a museum you enjoy visiting.

Activities: *(1) look at paintings (2) relax in the café (3) browse in the gift shop*

Description: *I enjoy looking at the paintings, but after a couple of hours of that, I usually feel tired. I like to relax for a short while in the café, drinking coffee and eating pastries. Before I go home, I like to spend a few minutes browsing in the gift shop. Sometimes I buy something, and sometimes I just look.*

PRACTICE

A. *For each topic and question, choose three activities to describe. Write one sentence about each one.*

B. *Then, without looking at your notes, answer the questions out loud. Record your answers and listen to them. Record your answers over and over until you are satisfied with your presentation.*

1.

Topic: A recent trip

Question: Describe some things you did on a recent trip.

Activities: _____

Description: _____

                _____

                _____

2.

Topic: A friend you spend time with

Question: Describe some activities you enjoy doing with a friend.

Activities: _____

Description: _____

_____

_____

3.

Topic: A holiday you enjoy

Question: Describe some things you do to celebrate a holiday you enjoy.

Activities: _____

Description: _____

_____

_____

Skill 2 Opinions

The first question in the Speaking section may ask for your personal opinion about a place, event, or activity. You will be asked to talk about something that is important to you, and you will have to explain *why* it is important.

Example

What type of class do you prefer to attend? Why?

Here are some words and phrases that are used for explaining *why*.

Useful words and phrases		
From my point of view	I feel that	If I had to choose
I agree that	I think that	In my opinion
I believe that	I would prefer to	To my mind

Tip	Remember that some questions ask for your opinion. In this case, pronouns like *I*, *me*, *my* are appropriate.

Example

Think of an important gift that you received recently, and explain the reason you received the gift and why it was important to you.

Opinion: *A watch is one of the most meaningful gifts I have ever received.*

Supporting Detail 1:   *graduation present*

Supporting Detail 2: *from my father*

Supporting Detail 3: *shows his pride in me*

Response

When I graduated from high school, my father gave me the gift of an expensive camera. I feel that this is one of the most meaningful gifts I have ever received. I received it for my high school graduation, which was an important turning point in my life. I received the gift from my father, who is very important to me and whose good opinion I always work hard to receive. My father gave me this expensive gift to show his pride in me, because I finished high school so successfully.

PRACTICE

A. Read the questions below. Make notes for your response. Use your notes to write a response for each question.

B. Then, without looking at your writing, answer the question out loud. Record your opinion and listen to it. Record your answer several times until you are satisfied with your presentation.

Notes

1. Choose a famous person you admire, and explain why you admire this person.

   Opinion: _____

   Supporting Detail 1: _____

   Supporting Detail 2: _____

   Supporting Detail 3: _____

2. Think of a place you would like to live, and explain why you would like to live there.

   Opinion: _____

   Supporting Detail 1: _____

   Supporting Detail 2: _____

   Supporting Detail 3: _____

3. Think of an expensive purchase you made recently, and explain why this purchase was important to you.

   Opinion: _____

   Supporting Detail 1: _____

   Supporting Detail 2: _____

   Supporting Detail 3: _____

4. Choose a friend you enjoy spending time with, and explain why this friend is important to you.

   Opinion: _____

   Supporting Detail 1: _____

   Supporting Detail 2: _____

   Supporting Detail 3: _____

Responses

1. _____

_____

_____

2. _____

_____

_____

3. _____

_____

_____

4. _____

_____

_____

Skill 3   Specific Information

When you give supporting details in the Speaking section, you should provide specific information. You do not want to be general.

General: It's a big campus.

Specific: It's the largest university campus in the region.

General: I like to study at night.

Specific: I prefer to study after dinner for about two hours.

Tip	When you provide specific information, you will often use superlatives. Review superlatives with –*est* and *most* as well as irregulars such as *the best, the worst.*

PRACTICE

Rewrite the following general statements. Make them more specific. When you are finished, look at your own Supporting Details in Skill 1. Can you make them more specific?

1. General: She's a fun person.

Specific: _____

2. General: It was an interesting movie.

Specific: _____

3. General: There's a lot to do near the university.

Specific: _____

4. General: I've lived in this neighborhood for a long time.

   Specific: _____

5. General: It was a very special gift.

   Specific: _____

Question 2   Personal Choice

Question 2 is a personal choice question. You will be asked to give your opinion again. This time you will be offered two choices. You will have to choose one and support your reason.

Tip	Remember to include reasons that support your opinion.

Skill 4   Compare and Contrast

By comparing and contrasting the two choices, you will be able to discuss *why* you prefer one choice.

Tip	When you compare and contrast, you will often use comparatives. Review comparatives with *–er* and *more* as well as irregulars such as *better, worse*.

Example

Some students prefer to study at a large university. Others prefer to study at a smaller university or college. Which type of school do you think is better, and why?

When you make your notes, you should make two columns and write how the choices are similar or different.

Similar	Different
higher education	number of students
	size of classes
	choice of courses

Then use the information in the column to write three general ideas. These ideas will be your "main ideas" for your response to Question 2.

General Idea: *Both kinds of schools offer higher education.*

General Idea: *Unlike large universities, smaller schools often have smaller classes.*

General Idea: *Larger schools have more courses to choose from.*

You will then need to add specific information to tell *why* you prefer one particular choice.

General Idea: *Both kinds of schools offer higher education.*

Specific Information: *They prepare students for a career.*

Specific Information: *They give students degrees.*

Here are some words and phrases that are used for comparing and contrasting.

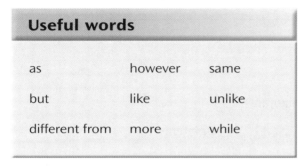

Useful words		
as	however	same
but	like	unlike
different from	more	while

Comparative and superlative adjectives are also used to compare and contrast.

Examples

Big colleges usually have larger classes than small colleges do.

Libraries at larger colleges often have more extensive collections of books.

The biggest colleges often have great sports teams.

PRACTICE

A. *Read the following questions. Make notes on how they are similar (compare) and how they are different (contrast). Then use your notes to write three general ideas for each question. Use compare and contrast words.*

B. *Without looking at your notes, answer the question out loud. Record your answers and listen to them. Record your answers several times until you are satisfied with your presentation.*

1. Question

On a weekend evening, would you prefer to go to a party or spend time with just a few close friends?

Similar   Different

_____   _____

_____   _____

_____   _____

General Idea: _____

General Idea: _____

General Idea: _____

2. Question

Would you prefer to live in a place that has four seasons, including a cold winter, or a place that has pleasant weather all year long?

Similar   Different

_____   _____

_____   _____

_____   _____

General Idea: _____

General Idea: _____

General Idea: _____

3. Question

Do you prefer to eat at home or at restaurants?

Similar   Different

_____   _____

_____   _____

_____   _____

General Idea: _____

General Idea: _____

General Idea: _____

4. Question

Would you prefer to live in an apartment or a house?

Similar   Different

_____   _____

_____   _____

_____   _____

General Idea: _____

General Idea: _____

General Idea: _____

Skill 5   Specific Explanations

Question 2 asks you to explain *why* you prefer one choice. As with Question 1, it is important to be specific.

Example

Some students prefer to study at a large university. Others prefer to study at a smaller university or college. Which type of school do you think is better, and why?

You will need to add specific information to tell *why* you prefer one particular choice.

General Idea: *Both kinds of schools offer higher education.*

Specific Information: *They prepare students for a career.*

Specific Information: *They give students degrees.*

General Idea: *Unlike large universities, smaller schools often have smaller classes.*

Specific Information: *Students get more individual attention.*

Specific Information: *For this reason, it's easier for students to participate in class discussions.*

General Idea: *Larger schools have more courses to choose from.*

Specific Information: *This can be good for students who have clear goals but confusing for students who don't.*

Specific Information: *Since a smaller school has fewer courses, students stay focused on their goals.*

 Tip Practice using different Useful words, but make sure you know the exact meaning when you use a word during the test.

Here are some words and phrases that are used for explaining *why*.

Useful words and phrases

another reason	since
because (of)	so
For this reason	that's why

PRACTICE

A. Give specific information for each general idea you wrote in Skill 4. Use explaining words.

B. Then, without looking at your notes, answer the questions out loud. Record your answers and listen to them. Record your answers several times until you are satisfied with your presentation.

1. General Idea: _____

Specific Information: _____

Specific Information: _____

General Idea: _____

Specific Information: _____

Specific Information: _____

General Idea: _____

Specific Information: _____

Specific Information: _____

2. General Idea: _____
Specific Information: _____
Specific Information: _____

General Idea: _____
Specific Information: _____
Specific Information: _____

General Idea: _____
Specific Information: _____
Specific Information: _____

3. General Idea: _____
Specific Information: _____
Specific Information: _____

General Idea: _____
Specific Information: _____
Specific Information: _____

General Idea: _____
Specific Information: _____
Specific Information: _____

4. General Idea: _____
Specific Information: _____
Specific Information: _____

General Idea: _____
Specific Information: _____
Specific Information: _____

General Idea: _____
Specific Information: _____
Specific Information: _____

Question 3   Campus Situation   Read/Listen/Speak

In Question 3, you will read an explanation on a subject and you will listen to a conversation or talk on the same subject. Then you will have to explain the speaker's opinion of the subject.

Skill 6   Point of View

In Question 3, you will have to listen for the speaker's opinion on the subject you read about. Then you will have to explain why the speaker has this point of view. Make notes as you listen.

Example

Directions

Read the passage. Listen to the conversation. Make notes. Then answer the question.

Read

Summer Cafeteria Schedule

Because there are fewer students on campus during the summer session, the hours that the cafeteria is open will be reduced. Breakfast will be served from 7:00 AM until 8:00 AM, lunch from 11:30 AM until 12:30 PM, and dinner from 5:30 PM until 6:30 PM. The afternoon coffee hour will be discontinued for the summer and will resume at the start of the fall semester. Meal tickets are available in the Office of Student Services and cost $300 for the three-meal plan for the summer session, and $6 each for individual meal tickets.

 Listen

Question

State the woman's opinion about the summer cafeteria schedule, and explain her reasons for her opinion.

First, clearly state the speaker's opinion. Then, as in Question 1, you can organize your notes in terms of general ideas with specific information as supporting details.

Note-taking

When you take notes, you want to save time, so don't write complete sentences. Write just key content words, omitting things such as articles and auxiliary verbs, for example, "woman needs to study for exam all weekend but has to work". The sample notes here are mainly complete sentences to aid you in planning for speaking.

Opinion: _The woman thinks the summer cafeteria schedule is a bad idea._

General Idea: _Breakfast is too early._

Specific Information: _Breakfast is over at 8:00._

Specific Information: _Her first class is at 10:00._

General Idea:	The schedule isn't good for students who work in the cafeteria.
Specific Information:	They will work fewer hours.
Specific Information:	In other words, they will earn less money.

General Idea:	The afternoon coffee hour will be cancelled.
Specific Information:	She likes coffee in the afternoon.
Specific Information:	She'll spend more money on coffee somewhere else.

Here are some words and phrases that are used for adding supporting details.

Useful words and phrases

also	for instance	in other words
but	however	in the first place
for example	in addition	more

PRACTICE

A. *Read the passages and listen to the conversations and short talks. Make notes for your response as you read and listen. Use your notes to write some sentences about each question.*

B. *Then, without looking at your writing, answer each question out loud. Record your answer and listen to it. Record your answer several times until you are satisfied with your presentation.*

 1.

Directions

Read the passage. Listen to the conversation. Make notes. Then answer the question.

Read

> **Sociology Class—Research Project**
>
> All students in this class are required to do a field research project. This means you will design a project that involves observing and/or interviewing subjects on campus or somewhere in the larger community. Your grade will be based on your ability to design a project, carry it out, and analyze the results. During the first half of the semester we will discuss project design, field research methods, and data analysis. The second part of the semester will be devoted to implementing your projects.

 Listen

Question

State the man's opinion about the sociology class requirement, and explain his reasons for his opinion.

Notes

Opinion: _____

General Idea: _____
Specific Information: _____
Specific Information: _____

General Idea: _____
Specific Information: _____
Specific Information: _____

General Idea: _____
Specific Information: _____
Specific Information: _____

🎧 2.

Directions

Read the passage. Listen to the conversation. Make notes. Then answer the question.

Read

Parking Lot Closure

During the month of April, the north student parking lot will be closed to repair the damage caused by last winter's storms. Since this will greatly reduce the number of parking spots available to students on campus, students are encouraged to seek alternative forms of transportation during this time. Cars with student parking stickers will not be allowed to park in faculty or visitor parking areas. We appreciate your cooperation and apologize for any inconvenience this may cause.

🎧 **Listen**

Question

State the woman's opinion about the restrictions on student parking, and explain her reasons for her opinion.

Notes

Opinion: _____

General Idea: _____
Specific Information: _____
Specific Information: _____

General Idea: _____

Specific Information: _____

Specific Information: _____

General Idea: _____

Specific Information: _____

Specific Information: _____

3.

Directions

Read the passage. Listen to the conversation. Make notes. Then answer the question.

Read

Pet Policy Reminder

This is a reminder that students are not allowed to keep pets in the dormitories. This means pets of any kind, including those kept in cages or aquariums. There have been numerous complaints recently about violations of this rule. Please be advised that any pets found in the dormitories will be confiscated and a fine will be imposed on the offending parties. Please leave your pets at home during the school year. Your cooperation is appreciated.

Listen

Question

State the man's opinion about the pet policy, and explain his reasons for his opinion.

Notes

Opinion: _____

General Idea: _____

Specific Information: _____

Specific Information: _____

General Idea: _____

Specific Information: _____

Specific Information: _____

General Idea: _____

Specific Information: _____

Specific Information: _____

4.

Directions

Read the passage. Listen to the conversation. Make notes. Then answer the question.

Read

Student Center Movies

The Student Council has elected to spend a portion of this year's entertainment budget on weekly movies. The movies will be shown in the Student Center on Tuesday nights at 7:30 PM. Admission is free and complimentary popcorn and drinks will be served. There will be a guided discussion following each movie for everyone who is interested. A schedule of the movies to be shown this semester will be posted soon on the Student Council website.

 Listen

Question

State the woman's opinion about the decision to show movies at the Student Center.

Notes

Opinion: _____

General Idea: _____

Specific Information: _____

Specific Information: _____

General Idea: _____

Specific Information: _____

Specific Information: _____

General Idea: _____

Specific Information: _____

Specific Information: _____

Question 4   Lecture   Read/Listen/Speak

For Question 4, you will read a passage similar to those in a college textbook. Then, as in a college classroom, you will listen to part of a lecture on the same topic. You will then respond to a question that asks the relationship between the passage and the lecture.

> **Tip** | All of the academic questions provide whatever information is needed to give a response. You are not expected to have any experience with the subject matter.

Skill 7   Determine the Purpose

For Question 4, you will be asked to determine the purpose of the lecture. You will be asked whether the lecture supports the passage, adds information to it, or contradicts it. Most of the tasks in Question 4 ask you how the lecture supports or adds more information to the passage.

> **Tip** | Listen for differences between the reading and listening passages, and make notes as soon as you hear a key similarity or a difference. Use your own notetaking symbols, such as = for "same" and – for "different".

Example

Directions

Read the passage. Listen to the lecture and make notes. Then answer the question.

Read

> Conformity has been the focus of a number of well-known social psychology experiments. The concept of conformity looks at the behavior of an individual in a group situation. Conformity is the process though which the individual adjusts his or her behavior and views to match those of the rest of the group. Conformity is part of our daily lives. When we sit facing the front rather than the back of the classroom, we are conforming. We are conforming when we drive on the correct side of the road. Conformity can also involve socially unacceptable behavior as, for example, when a peer group pressures members into drug use or other illegal actions.

 Listen

Question

The lecturer describes the Solomon Asch experiment. Explain how this experiment demonstrates the concept of conformity.

Sample Response

> *The lecturer talks about conformity. Conformity is when an individual in a group changes his or her behavior to be like the behavior of other members of the group. The lecturer describes the Solomon Asch experiment, which was a famous experiment about conformity done in the 1950s. In a group of eight people, only one was the study subject. The others were assistants. They were shown cards with lines drawn on them. They had to choose which line was as long as another line. It was easy to see the correct answer, but the assistants gave incorrect answers. One-third of the time, the study subject also gave the wrong answer. Instead of giving the correct answer, he conformed by giving the same answer as everyone else. So he matched his behavior to the rest of the group.*

Tip	Be sure to write down key names as soon as you hear them, so that you can use them in your response. Look quickly back at the question to check spelling.

PRACTICE

Read the passage and determine its purpose. Listen to the lecture and make notes about the details. Then answer the question.

1.

Read

> Many animal species rely on camouflage to survive in the wild. The coloring and markings of an animal's fur or skin help it to hide from predators if it is a prey animal, or from the prey it hunts if it is a predator.
>
> Camouflage works in different ways. *Blending*, for example, is when camouflage enables an animal to blend in with its surroundings, such as a white polar bear in the snow. *Pattern* is when an animal's markings make it difficult to discern the shape of the animal's body. Zebras' and tigers' stripes are examples of this type of camouflage.

Choose the statement that is most likely the purpose of this passage.

This passage

(A) suggests why zebras live in herds

(B) defines predators and prey

(C) describes how polar bears survive in the snow

(D) explains how coloring protects animals

 Listen

Write three details from the lecture that support, add to, or contradict the purpose of the passage.

Details

1. _____

2. _____

3. _____

Question

Explain how a zebra's stripes may help protect it.

2.

Read

Deviant behavior is behavior which goes against social norms, or rules. These norms may be formally-defined rules, such as a country's laws, and going against them would constitute a criminal act. Or, they may be generally accepted social conventions, for example, speaking quietly in a library, or shaking hands when meeting someone, in U.S. culture.

Sociologists have developed a number of theories around deviant behavior. The labeling theory focuses more on how society perceives and labels deviant behavior than on the deviant behavior itself. It suggests that a person becomes deviant when he or she is so labeled by society.

Choose the statement that is most likely the purpose of this passage.

This passage

(A) explains the reasons for engaging in deviant behavior

(B) discusses criminal acts as examples of deviant behavior

(C) defines deviant behavior and mentions one theory about it

(D) gives reasons to support the validity of one theory of deviant behavior

 Listen

Write three details from the lecture that support, add to, or contradict the purpose of the passage.

Details

1. _____

2. _____

3. _____

Question

The lecturer describes "The Saints and the Roughnecks" study. Explain what this study tells us about deviant behavior.

3.

Read

> The words *epidemic* and *pandemic* both refer to widespread outbreaks of disease. An epidemic occurs when a disease spreads throughout a community, infecting a larger number of people than would normally be expected. An epidemic is usually localized within a town or region. When it is more widespread, particularly when it spreads to several countries, then it becomes a pandemic. A pandemic is usually caused by a new type or strain of a disease, one that people have not yet developed an immunity for. With their high death tolls, pandemics can lead to high levels of economic loss and social disruption over wide areas of the world.

Tip Look for special printing called *italics* in a reading passage. Italics are used to mark special words and terms.

Choose the statement that is most likely the purpose of this passage.

This passage

(A) explains the causes of epidemics and pandemics

(B) defines the terms *epidemic* and *pandemic*

(C) describes some recent epidemics and pandemics

(D) suggest ways to prevent epidemics and pandemics

 Listen

Write three details from the lecture that support, add to, or contradict the purpose of the passage.

Details

1. _____

2. _____

3. _____

Question

Explain why the flu epidemic of 1918 can be considered to be a pandemic.

4.

Read

An *invasive* species can be defined as a species of animal or plant that does not naturally occur in a specific habitat, and whose presence upsets the natural balance in that habitat. Invasive species pose a threat because they push out native species. A species in an alien environment may lack natural competitors or predators. This gives it an advantage over the native species and allows it to take over space and resources that would otherwise be used by the native species. Invasive species can be introduced by natural processes or by human activity.

Choose the statement that is most likely the purpose of this passage.

This passage

(A) explains what invasive species are and why they are a problem

(B) suggests ways to combat the problem of invasive species

(C) tells which invasive species are the most problematic

(D) describes several examples of invasive species

 Listen

Write three details from the lecture that support, add to, or contradict the purpose of the passage.

Details

1. _____

2. _____

3. _____

Question

Explain how purple loosestrife is an example of an invasive species.

Question 5   Campus Situation   Listen/Speak

In Question 5, you will listen to conversations with two possible solutions to a problem. You will have to pick one of the solutions.

Skill 8 Problem/Solution

For Question 5, clearly identify the problem. Look for the advantages and disadvantages in each potential solution. Then choose the solution you think best. You will find the *compare and contrast* skills you learned in Skill 4 useful for Question 5.

Here are some words and phrases that are used for comparing and contrasting.

Useful words and phrases			
Comparison		**Contrast**	
also	like	although/even though	however
as. . . as	similar to	but	less/more
both	the same as	different from	on the other hand

Example

 Listen

Question

The woman has a problem, and the man suggests two possible solutions. Describe the problem and the two solutions. Explain which solution you prefer, and why.

Tip	When you take notes, you should leave out easily understood words like *a*, *an*, *the* and verbs like *is* or *are*. You can also leave out most pronouns because you will know who, or what, they refer to.

Notes

Problem: *The woman needs to spend all weekend studying for an exam, but she has to work at her job for part of the weekend.*

Solution 1:   *ask co-worker to work for her*

Advantages

friends like to help each other

Disadvantages

friend might be busy

supervisor might not like it

would lose work hours

Solution 2:   *ask supervisor to change schedule*

Advantages

wouldn't lose work hours

Disadvantages

supervisor might not agree

could get supervisor's approval

Response

> *The woman needs to spend all weekend studying for an exam, but she has to work at her job for part of the weekend. She wants to get out of working so she can study for her exam. One solution is to ask a friend to work for her. The other solution is to ask her supervisor to change the schedule, so that she can work after the exam is over instead of tomorrow. I think the second solution is the best option. Her friend might want to help her, but might not be available. Also, her supervisor might not like her to make changes without asking him first. If she asks the supervisor to change the schedule, on the other hand, then the supervisor has the chance to approve the change. In addition, she wouldn't lose any work hours, she would just be doing them at a different time.*

PRACTICE

A. *Listen to the problems and the two solutions. Make notes of the problem and the advantages and disadvantages of each solution.*

B. *Choose a solution, and write a response telling why you think this solution is better.*

 1. Listen

Question

The man has a problem with his economics class, and the woman suggests two possible solutions. Describe the problem and the two solutions. Explain which solution you prefer, and why.

Solution 1: _____

Advantages	Disadvantages
_____	_____
_____	_____

Solution 2: _____

Advantages	Disadvantages
_____	_____
_____	_____

Response

_____

_____

_____

_____

2. Listen

Question

The woman has a problem about the geology class field trip, and the man suggests two possible solutions. Describe the problem and the two solutions. Explain which solution you prefer, and why.

Solution 1: _____

Advantages   Disadvantages

_____   _____

_____   _____

Solution 2: _____

Advantages   Disadvantages

_____   _____

_____   _____

Response

_____

_____

_____

_____

3. Listen

Question

The two students discuss a problem with a scheduled speaker, as well as two possible solutions. Describe the problem and the two solutions. Explain which solution you prefer, and why.

Solution 1: _____

Advantages   Disadvantages

_____   _____

_____   _____

Solution 2: _____

Advantages   Disadvantages

_____   _____

_____   _____

Response

_____

_____

_____

_____

4. Listen

Question

The woman has a problem about her biology textbook, and the man suggests two possible solutions. Describe the problem and the two solutions. Explain which solution you prefer, and why.

Solution 1: _____

Advantages   Disadvantages

_____   _____

_____   _____

Solution 2: _____

Advantages   Disadvantages

_____   _____

_____   _____

Response

_____

_____

_____

_____

Question 6 Lecture Listen/Speak

In Question 6, you will have to listen to and then summarize a lecture. You will have to discuss in depth the arguments made by the professor.

Skill 9 Citing and Summarizing

For Question 6, it is important that you take good notes. You will have to remember the main ideas and the supporting details from the lecture. When you discuss the lecture, you will have to cite the lecturer (say what points the lecturer made) and summarize the lecture.

Here are some words and phrases that are used for organizing ideas.

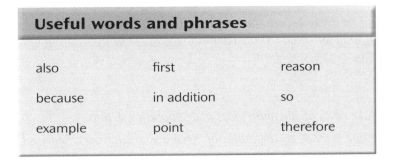

Useful words and phrases		
also	first	reason
because	in addition	so
example	point	therefore

Example

 Listen

Question

Use information from the lecture to explain why birds migrate.

> **Tip** Always practice taking notes in your own shorthand. But <u>remember</u>, your spoken responses must use full forms and complete sentences, not shorthand.

Notes

Main Idea A:	*reasons for bird migration*
Supporting Detail 1:	*difficult, so why do they do it?*
Supporting Detail 2:	*breeding*
Supporting Detail 3:	*feeding*

Main Idea B:	*summer in cold places*
Supporting Detail 1:	*a lot of daylight means more food*
Supporting Detail 2:	*cold winters mean few predators*

Main Idea C:	*winter in warm places*
Supporting Detail 1:	*food abundant year-round*
Supporting Detail 2:	*rest, eat, prepare for migration*

Response

> *The professor talks about the <u>reasons for bird migration. Migration is difficult for birds.</u> It takes a lot of energy and is risky, <u>so why do they do it?</u> The first reason the professor gives is <u>breeding</u>. The second reason is <u>feeding</u>.*
>
> *<u>Migratory birds spend summers in cold places</u> like the Arctic and Antarctic regions. In these places, there is <u>a lot of daylight in the summer and that means there is more food,</u> like plants and bugs. Birds can have larger families because there is more food for them. Also, <u>in places where the winters are cold, there are few predators. It's a safer place</u> to have babies.*
>
> *<u>Then the birds can fly</u> away before the winter comes. <u>They go to warm places because there is abundant food</u> for them to eat. They can <u>spend the winter eating and resting and then they are ready to migrate</u> again.*

PRACTICE

A. *Listen to the lecture. Make notes of the main ideas and supporting details.*

B. *Give a summary of the points made by the professor. Record your summary. Repeat it several times until you are satisfied with your presentation.*

 1. Listen

Question

Use information from the lecture to explain two ways that the saguaro cactus has adapted to desert conditions.

Main Idea A: _____

Supporting Detail 1: _____

Supporting Detail 2: _____

Main Idea B: _____

Supporting Detail 1: _____

Supporting Detail 2: _____

Main Idea C: _____

Supporting Detail 1: _____

Supporting Detail 2: _____

2. Listen

Question

Use information from the lecture to explain how the automobile has changed the American landscape.

Main Idea A: _____

Supporting Detail 1: _____

Supporting Detail 2: _____

Main Idea B: _____

Supporting Detail 1: _____

Supporting Detail 2: _____

Main Idea C: _____

Supporting Detail 1: _____

Supporting Detail 2: _____

3. Listen

Question

Use information from the lecture to describe the history of the potato in Europe.

Main Idea A: _____

Supporting Detail 1: _____

Supporting Detail 2: _____

Main Idea B: _____

Supporting Detail 1: _____

Supporting Detail 2: _____

Main Idea C: _____

Supporting Detail 1: _____

Supporting Detail 2: _____

4. Listen

Question

Use information from the lecture to describe how Impressionist artists painted differently from artists before them.

Main Idea A: _____

Supporting Detail 1: _____

Supporting Detail 2: _____

Main Idea B: _____

Supporting Detail 1: _____

Supporting Detail 2: _____

Main Idea C: _____

Supporting Detail 1: _____

Supporting Detail 2: _____

General Speaking Skills

Skill 10   Word Families and Stress

Learning about and using word families increases your vocabulary and your fluency in English. In addition to knowing the meanings of word families, you also need to know how to pronounce each word correctly. Depending on what suffixes you add to a root word, the stress may or may not shift.

Some suffixes cause no change in stress.

-able	be**lieve**—be**liev**able
-ive	cre**ate**—cre**ati**ve
-ful	**mean**ing—**mean**ingful
-less	**mean**ing—**mean**ingless
-ment	ex**cite**—ex**cite**ment
-ize	**mo**tor—**mo**torize
-ly	**ea**sy—**ea**sily

Some suffixes cause the stress to shift to the syllable immediately preceding the suffix.

-ity	**hu**man—hu**man**ity
-ic	**elec**tron—elec**tron**ic
-ify	**a**cid—a**cid**ify
-ical	e**co**nomy—eco**nom**ical
-ian	**his**tory—his**tor**ian

Some suffixes cause the stress to shift to the first syllable of the suffix.

-ation/-ition/-ution	de**clare**—decla**ra**tion
-etic	**en**ergy—ener**ge**tic

PRACTICE

Look at these word families. Say the words aloud. Underline the stressed syllable in each word. Say the words aloud again.

	Root Word	Noun	Verb	Adjective	Adverb
1.	inform	information	inform	informative	informatively
2.	believe	belief	believe	believable	believably
3.	adore	adoration	adore	adorable	adorably
4.	argue	argument	argue	arguable	arguably
5.	attract	attraction	attract	attractive	attractively
6.	master	mastery	master	masterful	masterfully
7.	simple	simplification	simplify	simple	simply
8.	rhetoric	rhetoric		rhetorical	rhetorically
9.	sense	sense	sense/sensitize	sensitive	sensitively
10.	apathy	apathy		apathetic	apathetically

Skill 11   Sentence Stress

Some words in a sentence carry meaning. Other words are function words. The stress is usually on the words that carry meaning, not on the function words.

Meaning	Function
adjectives	articles
nouns	auxiliaries
question words	conjunctions
verbs	prepositions
	pronouns
	relative pronouns

Examples

I prefer movies that have a lot of **action**.

I enjoy winter sports, such as **skiing** and **snowboarding.**

An **apartment** can be as **comfortable** as a **house**.

PRACTICE

Read each sentence aloud. Underline the stressed words. Then read the sentence aloud again.

1. The students feel that the class assignment is too difficult.

2. It isn't easy to find a place to park on campus.

3. If he doesn't study harder, he could get a failing grade.

4. The food in a restaurant is usually delicious, but often expensive.

5. There are still many questions about bird migration.

Skill 12   Transition Words and Intonation

A transition word has a rising intonation. The end of the sentence or clause has a falling intonation.

In addition, some pets make a lot of noise.

Furthermore, I can take the computer with me wherever I go.

We have been going there for holidays since I was very young.

PRACTICE

Read each sentence aloud. Mark the intonation patterns for transition words. Then read the sentence aloud again.

1. First, the student parking regulations aren't fair.

2. However, the man doesn't agree with the woman's opinion.

3. She's had this problem since the semester began, I think.

4. On the other hand, winter is a very beautiful time of year.

5. Nevertheless, many people aren't aware of her accomplishments.

Skill 13   Lists and Intonation

Lists have a specific stress pattern. There is rising intonation on the first words of a list and falling intonation on the last word.

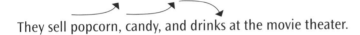

They sell popcorn, candy, and drinks at the movie theater.

This semester I'm studying biology, chemistry, physics, and math.

PRACTICE 1

Read each sentence aloud. Mark the intonation pattern, then read the sentence aloud again.

1. Summer weather is hot, humid, and uncomfortable.

2. At a restaurant you just order, eat, pay, and then go home.

3. In this class we have to do research, write reports, and take exams.

4. She needs money for tuition, books, and housing.

5. Apartments are generally small, comfortable, and inexpensive.

PRACTICE 2

Question 1

Read the question about a familiar topic. You have 15 seconds to prepare your response and 45 seconds to respond.

> Think of a neighborhood you know that you would like to live in. Explain why you would like to live there. Give reasons and specific details in your answer.

Question 2

Read the question asking for your opinion on a familiar topic. You have 15 seconds to prepare your response and 45 seconds to respond.

> Do you think it is better to own a car or use public transportation? Why?

Question 3

Read the passage. You have 45 seconds.

Notice

Starting next semester, the university library will impose fines on students for books and other library materials returned past the due date. We regret the necessity of this change in policy, but the honor system that is currently in place is no longer effective. Too many library materials have remained checked out for unacceptable periods of time, and many materials are permanently missing. The check-out times will stay the same: two weeks for books, one week for magazines, journals, CDs, and DVDs. Fines will be ten cents a day for all materials. Again, we regret the necessity of this policy and appreciate the cooperation of all students, faculty, and staff.

 Listen to the conversation.

Answer the question. You have 30 seconds to prepare your response and 60 seconds to respond.

> State the woman's opinion about the new library policy regarding overdue books, and explain her reasons for her opinion.

Question 4

Read the passage about phobias. You have 45 seconds.

A *phobia* is an extreme, irrational fear of something. It may be fear of a situation, of an activity, or of a specific object or animal. Phobias are more than the minor, everyday fears which most of us experience. They cause heightened anxiety, physical reactions such as shaking, rapid heartbeat, and shortness of breath, and can be so disabling that they interfere with the sufferer's ability to live a normal life. Some common phobias are: claustrophobia (fear of enclosed spaces), acrophobia (fear of heights), and aviophobia (fear of flying).

 Listen to the lecture.

Answer the question. You have 30 seconds to prepare your response and 60 seconds to respond.

> What is a phobia, and what are some treatments?

Question 5

 Listen to the conversation. Then answer the question. You have 20 seconds to prepare your response and 60 seconds to respond.

> The man has a problem regarding his apartment and the woman suggests two possible solutions. Describe the problem and the two solutions. Explain which solution you prefer, and why.

Question 6

 Listen to the lecture. Then answer the question. You have 20 seconds to prepare your response and 60 seconds to respond.

Use information from the lecture to describe the effects of the cotton gin on the U.S. economy.

SPEAKING PRACTICE TEST

Question 1

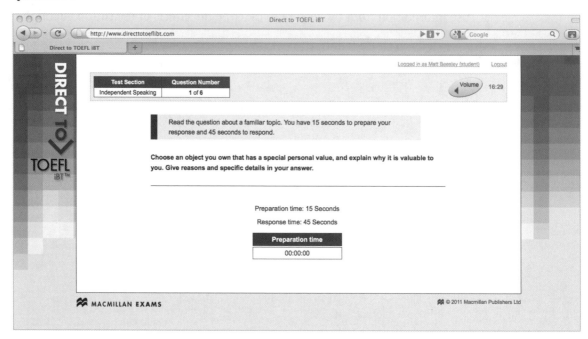

Question 2

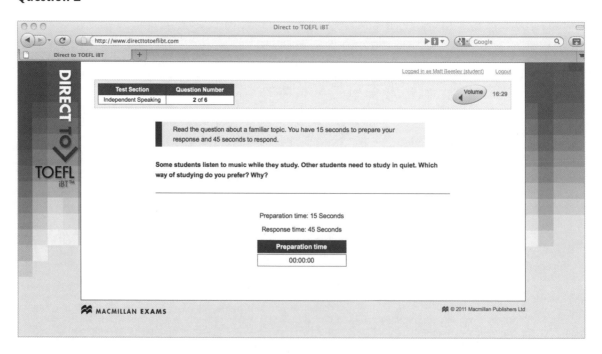

DIRECT TO TOEFL iBT™

Question 3

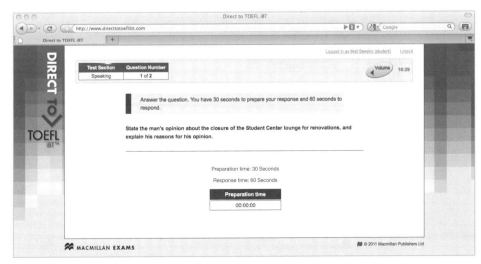

Question 4

The first screen reads:

Read the passage about the *bystander effect*. You have 45 seconds.

The *bystander effect* is the term used to describe the phenomenon whereby witnesses to an emergency situation fail to offer help because there are other people present. Attention became focused on this phenomenon following an incident which occurred in New York City in 1964. A woman, Kitty Genovese, was brutally attacked in front of her apartment building while her neighbors ignored her cries for help. Since then, research has shown that witnesses who are in the presence of others respond to an emergency situation only about 50% of the time, while lone witnesses have a 75% response rate.

The second screen reads:

Listen to the lecture.

The third screen reads:

Answer the question. You have 30 seconds to prepare your response and 60 seconds to respond.

The lecturer describes research by Darley and Latane. Explain how this research demonstrates the *bystander effect*.

Preparation time: 30 Seconds

Response time: 60 Seconds

Preparation time
00:00:00

Question 5

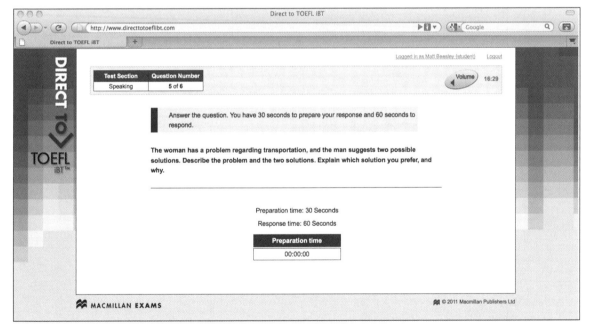

Question 6

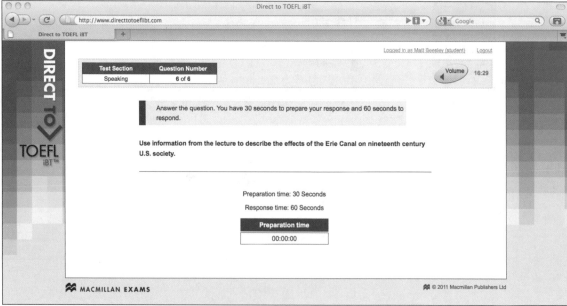

WRITING

Facts About Writing Skills

Integrated Writing Task

Skill 1   Main Ideas
Skill 2   Presenting the Information
Skill 3   Introduction
Skill 4   Adding Details
Skill 5   Summarizing the Points
Skill 6   Citing and Paraphrasing

Independent Writing Task

Skill 1   The Main Idea–Your Opinion
Skill 2   Writing the Introduction
Skill 3   Writing a Paragraph
Skill 4   Stating Your Opinion
               Expressing Your Opinion
               Generalizing and Qualifying
Skill 5   Putting it All Together

General Writing

Skill 1   Transition Words and Phrases
Skill 2   Synonyms
Skill 3   Pronouns
Skill 4   Parallel Structures
Skill 5   Coherence
               Repeating and Rephrasing
Skill 6   Sentence Types
Skill 7   Punctuation
Skill 8   Revision

Skills Practice

Writing Practice Test

The Writing section of the TOEFL iBT™ includes two writing tasks.

The first of these is an **Integrated Writing Task**. This task integrates reading, listening, and writing. You will first read an academic passage and then listen to a professor discussing the same topic in a lecture. The lecture will provide new information that either challenges or supports the information in the reading passage. In your essay, you must summarize the main points in the lecture and show how they relate to the reading passage.

You may take notes on both the reading passage and the lecture. You will then use your notes to organize your response. Your essay for the Integrated Writing Task should be about 150–225 words. You may write more, but you will only have 20 minutes to plan, write, and edit your response. Your essay will be scored on how well you present the main points in the lecture and their relationship to the reading passage.

The second task in Writing is an **Independent Writing Task**. For this task, you will write from your own experience. You will write a response to a question about an issue. You must support your opinions and choices with reasons and examples.

Your essay for the Independent Writing Task should be about 300 words long. You may write more, but you will only have 30 minutes to plan, write, and edit your response. There is no "right" or "wrong" answer to the question. Instead, your essay will be scored on how well you present and support your ideas.

The chart on page 193 shows you how the Integrated and Independent writing tasks compare. Pages 194–195 show you examples of what the screens look like for the two writing tasks.

You will have a total of 50 minutes to complete the two tasks in the Writing section. You will type your two essays on a computer. Your essays will be sent by computer to a scoring center, where they will be rated.

Facts About Writing

Integrated Task	**Read/Listen/Write**
Content	Academic topic
Length	230–300 word reading passage (3 minutes to read)
	230–300 word listening passage (2 minutes to listen)
Task	Write 150–225 words or more
Question	Summarize important points in listening passage as related to key points in reading passage
Time	20 minutes

Independent Task	**Write**
Content	Writing from experience and knowledge
Task	Write 300 words or more
Question	State, explain, and support your opinion on an issue
Time	30 minutes

Measures ability to	Select information from the lecture
	Express information coherently
	Organize the essay
	Address the topic and task
	Display unity and coherence
	Demonstrate variety with grammar structures and vocabulary

Sample Writing Screens

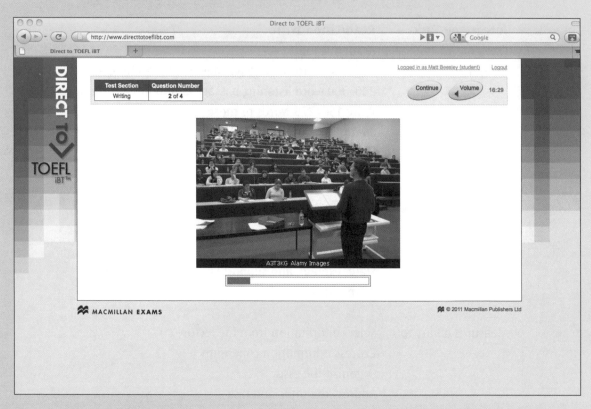

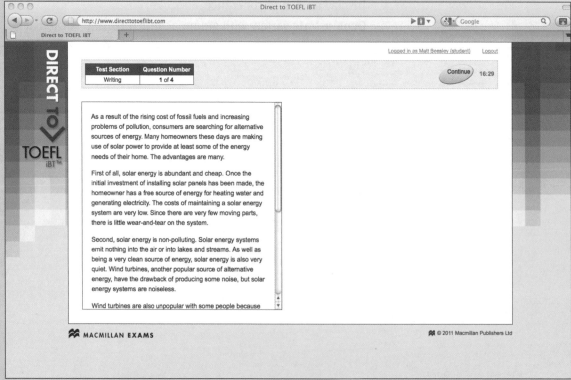

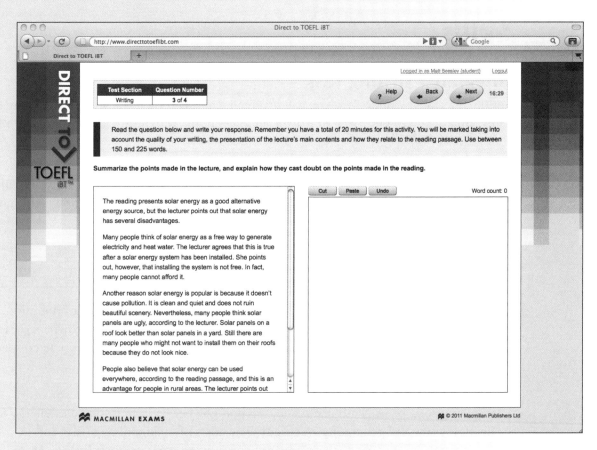

The reading presents solar energy as a good alternative energy source, but the lecturer points out that solar energy has several disadvantages.

Many people think of solar energy as a free way to generate electricity and heat water. The lecturer agrees that this is true after a solar energy system has been installed. She points out, however, that installing the system is not free. In fact, many people cannot afford it.

Another reason solar energy is popular is because it doesn't cause pollution. It is clean and quiet and does not ruin beautiful scenery. Nevertheless, many people think solar panels are ugly, according to the lecturer. Solar panels on a roof look better than solar panels in a yard. Still there are many people who might not want to install them on their roofs because they do not look nice.

People also believe that solar energy can be used everywhere, according to the reading passage, and this is an advantage for people in rural areas. The lecturer points out

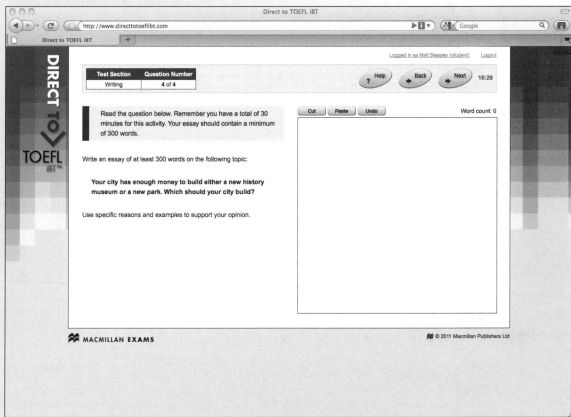

Skills

Integrated Writing Task

For the Integrated Writing Task, you will first read a passage. Then you will hear a lecture on the same subject. You will be asked to write a summary of the two, showing how they contrast or how they support each other.

Skill 1   Main Ideas

For the Integrated Writing Task, you will need to be able to identify the main ideas in both the reading passage and the lecture. You should practice identifying main ideas and taking notes as you read and as you listen.

Example

Read this passage and take notes on the main ideas.

> As a result of the rising cost of fossil fuels and increasing problems of pollution, consumers are searching for alternative sources of energy. Many homeowners these days are making use of solar power to provide at least some of the energy needs of their home. The advantages are many.
>
> First of all, solar energy is abundant and cheap. Once the initial investment of installing solar panels has been made, the homeowner has a free source of energy for heating water and generating electricity. The costs of maintaining a solar energy system are very low. Since there are very few moving parts, there is little wear-and-tear on the system.
>
> Second, solar energy is non-polluting. Solar energy systems emit nothing into the air or into lakes and streams. As well as being a very clean source of energy, solar energy is also very quiet. Wind turbines, another popular source of alternative energy, have the drawback of producing some noise, but solar energy systems are noiseless. Wind turbines are also unpopular with some people because they can spoil an otherwise beautiful landscape. Solar panels, on the other hand, can be installed so that they lie flat on a roof and are barely noticeable except from close up.
>
> A third advantage to solar power is that it can be used anywhere. This is especially important in rural areas where homes may be far from the already established power grid. Installing solar panels is an alternative to paying the costs of having the power company connect a remote house to the power grid.
>
> Today, in many places, homeowners are turning to solar power as an inexpensive and effective source of cheap, clean energy.

 Now listen to the lecture and take notes on the main ideas.

Tip	You should use your own shorthand when you take notes. Don't try to write complete sentences. These sample notes are written in shorthand so that you can see how you can take notes.

DIRECT TO TOEFL iBT™

Notes

Reading	Lecture
Main Ideas	Main Ideas
1. solar energy abundant and cheap	1. expensive to install system
2. doesn't cause pollution	2. can't be used everywhere
3. available everywhere	3. solar panels don't look nice

Practice

Read the passage and take notes. Then listen to the lecture and take notes. Use the spaces provided for your notes.

1. Read Passage 1 and take notes.

Reading
Main ideas

Lecture
Main ideas

THERE is a HIGH CORRELATION BETWEEN STUDENT ACHI.
THATS DEPEND of SEVERAL FACTORS AS PARENTS ACTITUDS
SCHOOL CAN BE do SEVERAL EFFECTS F-2 IMPROVE IT.

Passage 1

It is widely accepted that parental involvement in education has a positive effect on student achievement. Higher levels of parental involvement are associated with lower drop-out rates and improved academic performance. Consequently, schools invest significant time and resources into promoting the involvement of parents in their children's education.

Parental involvement can occur at several levels. At the school level, it can manifest itself as parental participation in school events of various types. These might include open-house nights, meetings with teachers, or performances and exhibits put on by students. It could also include volunteering in the classroom or at special events, such as school fairs and field trips.

At the home level, parental involvement can take diverse forms. On one hand, parents can demonstrate an active interest in their children's school activities. Parents can inquire about what their children are doing in class and what things generally are happening at school. Parents can also spend time every day going over homework assignments with their children. In addition, parents can involve their children in educational activities that support what they are doing in school. For example, parents and children can spend time reading together, and they can visit museums and local places of historical or cultural significance. In addition to supporting the development of specific skills and knowledge, such activities show that the family places a high value on education, thus strengthening a student's motivation and sense of achievement.

 Now listen to Lecture 1 and take notes.

2. Read Passage 2 and take notes.

Reading

Main ideas

Lecture

Main ideas

_____   _____

_____   _____

_____   _____

Passage 2

Aromatherapy is a popular alternative healing method. It makes use of naturally occurring aromatic compounds to treat certain health conditions, as well as to help people relax and improve mood. Essential oils are distilled from aromatic herbs, the most common of which are lemon, lavender, rosemary, and peppermint.

Aromatherapists claim that essential oils have a pharmacological effect similar to that of other types of medicines. The oils reportedly work to kill bacteria and viruses and stimulate the immune system. Many European doctors routinely include essential oils as part of patient treatment, most often for the oils' antibacterial, antiviral, and antifungal properties, as well as to ease headaches and other pains.

Aromatherapy is commonly employed as a mood enhancer. Massage therapists frequently incorporate various essential oils into their treatments, not only because the oils soothe aching muscles, but also because they reduce stress and help patients relax. Specific aromas are used for patients suffering from stress, anxiety, or insomnia. Aromatherapy is also used in the treatment of depression. Lavender, which produces a sense of well-being, is the essential oil most widely used to improve mood.

Essential oils can be delivered to the patient in a number of ways. One method is to diffuse the oil into the air. Another common method is for the patient to inhale the aroma directly as it evaporates from the oil. This method of delivery is useful for respiratory ailments, as well as for mood enhancement. Essential oils can also be applied directly to the skin. This direct method is commonly used for skin ailments and for stress-relieving massages. However, the essential oils need to be diluted with a carrier oil, such as almond or olive oil, otherwise damage to the skin may result.

Aromatherapy has proven to be a popular form of treatment for both psychological and physical ailments.

 Now listen to Lecture 2 and take notes.

3. Read Passage 3 and take notes.

Reading   Lecture

Main ideas   Main ideas

_____   _____

_____   _____

_____   _____

Passage 3

Forest fires can have natural or human causes. Lightning strikes are the most common natural cause. Human causes include activities, such as campfires, smoking, trash-burning, and other events. In order to burn, a forest fire requires three important elements: heat, oxygen, and fuel. Forest fires are frequently classified by the level of the forest in which they burn.

Ground fires burn at or below ground level, where there is low-lying vegetation and decaying organic matter. They are fueled by roots, decaying leaves, and other rotting vegetative matter. They are often smoldering fires and can burn slowly over a long period of time. They can even burn beneath the snow, and then flare up in the spring when the snow melts.

Surface fires are fires that burn from the ground level up to about ten feet high. They are fueled by timber litter, shrubs, and grasses. Certain trees have adaptations that protect them from surface fires. Douglas fir and ponderosa pine, for example, have their branches higher up, above the level where surface fires burn. They also have very thick bark which protects their trunks from the high heat of surface fires.

Crown fires burn at the highest level of the forest—the crowns of the trees. They are the most dangerous and destructive of forest fires. Crown fires can be the result of surface fires that have escalated. Crown fires can burn independently, jumping from crown to crown. For this reason, they can spread very rapidly, virtually exploding over large areas of forest in moments.

 Now listen to Lecture 3 and take notes.

4. Read Passage 4 and take notes.

Reading   Lecture
Main ideas   Main ideas

_____   _____

_____   _____

_____   _____

Passage 4

Industrial agriculture approaches food production in much the same way a factory approaches the production of manufactured goods. The goal is to produce the largest amount at the lowest possible cost. Industrial agriculture relies on a system of monoculture, devoting large pieces of land to a single crop. This system leads to a reliance on chemicals to maintain the high crop yields that are desired. Because of heavy chemical use, industrial agriculture is creating an environmental disaster.

Growing the same crop on the same piece of land year after year leads to several problems. One of these is that it attracts pests. If a favorite food source is always available, insects that feed on it will naturally show up in large numbers. The only means of controlling these pests is through the application of chemical pesticides. This practice puts poisons into the natural environment which pollute water, kill beneficial insects and other animals, and may cause disease in humans. Pesticides can also affect the natural fertility of the soil.

Growing the same crop in the same place year after year, instead of rotating crops or allowing sections to lie fallow, results in soil depletion. The natural nutrients in the soil are used up, so chemical fertilizers need to be applied. The application of fertilizers results in pollution, destroying the balance of the natural environment.

Industrial farming generally relies on only a few varieties of a plant. For example, in the 1990s, almost half the corn crop in the United States consisted of just six varieties of corn, while almost the entire pea crop consisted of just two varieties. Devoting large pieces of land to just one or two varieties of a crop makes those crops particularly susceptible to disease. This makes the application of chemicals necessary and can also lead to the loss of entire crops.

 Now listen to Lecture 4 and take notes.

Skill 2   Presenting the Information

Your task is to show how information in the lecture challenges or supports information in the reading. You should NOT give your opinion. You should only compare and contrast the main ideas of the reading passage with those of the lecture.

Lecture challenges the reading

> ➢ How are the main ideas different?

> ➢ Do they challenge the ideas in the reading?

> ➢ Do they answer problems in the reading?

Lecture supports the reading

> ➢ How are the main ideas similar?

> ➢ Do they support the reading?

> ➢ Do they add more information to the reading?

Example

In the reading passage and lecture on solar energy from Skill 1, the information in the lecture challenges the information in the reading.

Reading | Lecture
Main Ideas | Main Ideas

1. solar energy abundant and cheap ——— 1. expensive to install system

2. doesn't cause pollution ⟍ ⟋ 2. can't be used everywhere

3. available everywhere ——— 3. solar panels don't look nice

- **How are the main ideas different?** The reading passage discussed the advantages of using solar energy, and the lecture discusses the disadvantages.

- **Do they challenge the ideas in the reading?** The lecture challenges the ideas in the reading passage by pointing out the problems with solar energy.

- **Do they answer problems in the reading?** No, there are no problems presented in the reading passage.

| **Tip** | Remember: the verbs *challenge* and *support* have opposite meanings. When you see *challenge*, you will have to show how the two disagree. When you see *support*, you will have to show how they agree. The phrase *cast doubt on* is similar in meaning to *challenge*. |

Practice

Go back to your notes in Skill 1. Read the questions below for each reading passage and lecture. Draw a line in your notes between the ideas in the lecture and the ideas in the reading that support <u>or</u> challenge the reading. Not all ideas will be connected.

Example

Question: Summarize the points made in the lecture, and explain how they challenge the points made in the reading.

Reading	Lecture
Main Ideas	Main Ideas
1. solar energy abundant and cheap	1. expensive to install system
2. doesn't cause pollution	2. can't be used everywhere
3. available everywhere	3. solar panels don't look nice

1. Reading 1 and Lecture 1

   Question: Summarize the points made in the lecture, and explain how they strengthen the points made in the reading.

2. Reading 2 and Lecture 2

   Question: Summarize the points made in the lecture, and explain how they cast doubt on the points made in the reading.

3. Reading 3 and Lecture 3

   Question: Summarize the points made in the lecture, and explain how they support the points made in the reading.

4. Reading 4 and Lecture 4

   Question: Summarize the points made in the lecture, and explain how they answer the problems described in the reading.

Skill 3   Introduction

In the Introduction to your essay, you must tell the reader what you plan to say. You must describe in one or two sentences whether the lecture challenges or supports the reading passage. Look at the sample notes from the topic on solar energy:

Reading	Lecture
Main Ideas	Main Ideas
1. solar energy abundant and cheap	1. expensive to install system
2. doesn't cause pollution	2. can't be used everywhere
3. available everywhere	3. solar panels don't look nice

Look at a sample introduction for this topic:

The reading presents solar energy as a good alternative energy source, but the lecturer points out that solar energy has several disadvantages.

Here are some words that you can use to discuss a challenge or a support of the reading passage.

Useful words

Challenge	Support
but	agree
challenge	also
contradict	and
disagree	both
however	confirm
on the other hand	likewise
	support

Practice

Go back to the ideas that you connected in Skill 1. Choose the best introductory sentence for each set of notes.

1. Reading 1 and Lecture 1

   (A) The reading passage discusses the importance of parental involvement in education. The lecturer agrees that parental involvement is important and discusses ways to encourage it.

   (B) Schools should encourage parental involvement because it leads to higher student achievement.

2. Reading 2 and Lecture 2

   (A) The reading passage explains how aromatherapy has been used like medicine to treat illness and improve mood. The lecturer, however, says that there is no scientific evidence to prove that aromatherapy is effective.

   (B) The reading passage explains different ways that aromatherapy is used for different types of ailments. There are many people who do not believe in these kinds of treatments.

3. Reading 3 and Lecture 3

   (A) The lecturer explains that forest fires often have natural causes, such as lightning. They are important in maintaining the natural balance of forests.

   (B) Both the reading passage and the lecturer talk about the causes of forest fires and the different types of forest fires that can occur.

4. Reading 4 and Lecture 4

   (A) Industrial agricultural gets a high yield by using a system of monoculture. Unfortunately, it requires the heavy use of chemicals, and this has led to an environmental disaster.

   (B) Industrial agriculture relies on a system of monoculture to get high crop yields, which leads to the heavy use of chemicals. Organic farming, on the other hand, works with natural resources and does not require the use of chemicals.

Skill 4 Adding Details

You need to add supporting details to your discussion. These details will prove that you understand the reading and the lecture, and can write a coherent summary of the discussion.

Tip	Always look for the main idea in each paragraph. It is most often in the first sentence. The main idea is then followed by one or more details and/or examples.

Look at this example from the topic on solar energy:

Reading

Main Idea

Solar energy is abundant and cheap.

Supporting Details

free source of energy for heating water

free source of energy for generating electricity

Main Idea

Solar energy doesn't cause pollution.

Supporting Details

clean

quiet

doesn't ruin the landscape

Main Idea

Solar energy is available everywhere.

Supporting Details

advantage for people in rural areas

Lecture

Main Idea

It's expensive to install a solar energy system.

Supporting Details

many people can't afford

Main Idea

Solar energy cannot be used everywhere.

Supporting Details

useful in areas with a lot of sunshine

not useful in northern or rainy areas

Main Idea

Solar panels don't look nice to some people.

Supporting Details

panels on roof look better than in yard

many don't want panels on roof

Practice

Reread the passages and listen to the lectures again in Skill 1. Complete the notes below with Supporting Details. The numbered lines tell you how many details to look for.

1. Reading 1 and Lecture 1

Reading

Main Idea

Parental involvement in education is important.

Supporting Details

1. _____
2. _____
3. _____

Main Idea

Parents can be involved in different ways at school.

Supporting Details

1. _____
2. _____

Main Idea

Parents can be involved in different ways at home.

Supporting Details

1. _____
2. _____

Lecture

Main Idea

The attitude of teachers can discourage or encourage parental involvement.

Supporting Details

1. SOME TEACHER ARE AGREE AND HELP
2. THE TEACHER CREAT SOME opportunites

Main Idea

Parents might have difficulties that are barriers to involvement in education.

Supporting Details

1. FIELD TRIPS
2. HOMEWORK WITH THE CHILDREN.

Main Idea

Schools should work to encourage parental involvement because it is very important.

Supporting Details

1. NEED TRANED TO IMPROVE.
2. ORGANICE EVETS MEATINS FOR BUSY PARENTS
3. VOLUNTARIES, OR HOMEWORK

2. Reading 2 and Lecture 2

Reading	Lecture
Main Idea	**Main Idea**

Reading

Main Idea

Aromatherapy is an effective method for healing health conditions and improving mood.

Supporting Details

1. claim THE essencial oils HAVE A pitterntbyal effect
2. is commonly employed as a mood enhancer

Main Idea

Essential oils can be used like medicines.

Supporting Details

1. reportly used to kill bacterias or virus
2. Some doc. appli use them for anti bacterial antiviral ✓

Main Idea

Aromatherapy is used to enhance mood and relieve stress, anxiety, insomnia, and depression.

Supporting Details

1. Lavender produce sence of well-being
2. Essential oils can be delivered or different ways.

Lecture

Main Idea

There is no evidence to prove that aromatherapy is effective.

Supporting Details

1. No showed in scientist studies

Main Idea

A research study tested the effect of essential oils.

Supporting Details

1. Treatean of pain
2. Lemon and Lavender
3. tested in foots

Main Idea

There was little or no effect.

Supporting Details

1. have no effects on pain, mood etc
2. lavender: can be peel better

3. Reading 3 and Lecture 3

Reading

Main Idea

There are both natural and human causes of forest fires.

Supporting Details

1. _____
2. _____

Main Idea

Ground fires burn at or below ground level.

Supporting Details

1. _____
2. _____

Main Idea

Surface fires burn from the ground up to ten feet high.

Supporting Details

1. _____
2. _____

Main Idea

Crown fires burn at the tops of the trees.

Supporting Details

1. _____
2. _____
3. _____

Lecture

Main Idea

Forest fires caused by lightning are part of the balance of nature.

Supporting Details

1. _____
2. _____

Main Idea

Ground fires are usually controlled with trenches.

Supporting Details

1. _____
2. _____

Main Idea

Surface fires are controlled with water.

Supporting Details

1. _____
2. _____

Main Idea

Crown fires are controlled from the air.

Supporting Details

1. _____
2. _____

4. Reading 4 and Lecture 4

Reading

Main Idea

Industrial agriculture relies on monoculture for high crop yields.

Supporting Details

1. _____

2. _____

Main Idea

Planting the same crop in the same place every year attracts pests.

Supporting Details

1. _____

2. _____

Main Idea

Planting the same crop in the same place every year depletes the soil.

Supporting Details

1. _____

2. _____

Main Idea

In industrial farming, just a few varieties of a plant are grown.

Supporting Details

1. _____

2. _____

3. _____

Lecture

Main Idea

Organic farming works with natural resources, not chemicals.

Supporting Details

1. _____

Main Idea

Different methods are used for pest control.

Supporting Details

1. _____

2. _____

Main Idea

Healthy soil is important for healthy crops.

Supporting Details

1. _____

2. _____

3. _____

Main Idea

Different methods are used for disease control.

Supporting Details

1. _____

2. _____

Skill 5   Summarizing the Points

To write the integrated essay, you have to understand the main points in both the lecture and the reading. You have to know the relationship of the lecture to the reading. You have to summarize the main points. Look at this essay on the topic of solar energy, and compare it with the example outline in Skill 4.

Example

Question: Summarize the points made in the lecture, and explain how they cast doubt on the points made in the reading.

The reading presents solar energy as a good alternative energy source, but the lecturer points out that solar energy has several disadvantages.

Many people think of solar energy as a free way to generate electricity and heat water. The lecturer agrees that this is true after a solar energy system has been installed. She points out, however, that installing the system is not free. In fact, many people cannot afford it.

Another reason solar energy is popular is because it doesn't cause pollution. It is clean and quiet and does not ruin beautiful scenery. Nevertheless, many people think solar panels are ugly, according to the lecturer. Solar panels on a roof look better than solar panels in a yard. Still there are many people who might not want to install them on their roofs because they do not look nice.

People also believe that solar energy can be used everywhere, according to the reading passage, and this is an advantage for people in rural areas. The lecturer points out that this is not completely true. Although solar energy is useful in places that have a lot of sunshine, it is difficult to use in northern areas and rainy regions. The lecturer believes that solar energy is a good alternative energy source in some situations, but not in all.

These transition words will help you when you write your summaries.

Useful words and phrases	
Challenge	**Support**
although	also
challenge	another
conversely	as well
however	both
nevertheless	likewise
on the other hand	in addition
	support

Practice

Read each question. Then write a 150–225 word essay summarizing your notes from Skill 4.
Don't forget your introduction. Use a separate sheet of paper, or write on a computer.

1. **Topic:**   Parental Involvement

   Question: Summarize the points made in the lecture and explain how they strengthen the points made in the reading.

2. **Topic:**   Does Aromatherapy Work?

   Question: Summarize the points made in the lecture and explain how they challenge the points made in the reading.

3. **Topic:**   Forest Fires

   Question: Summarize the points made in the lecture and explain how they support the points made in the reading.

4. **Topic:**   Industrial Agriculture and Organic Farming

   Question: Summarize the points made in the lecture and explain how they answer the problems described in the reading.

Skill 6   Citing and Paraphrasing

For most responses on the Direct to TOEFL iBT™, you will use indirect quotes or paraphrase to refer to the author's or the lecturer's points. When you use the words of the author or lecturer, you should cite the author or speaker to let the reader know where the ideas originated.

A direct quote is the author's exact words; it uses quotation marks ("..."). An indirect quote uses a clause, often with *says that*. A paraphrase has the same meaning, but uses different grammatical structures and different vocabulary. Compare these examples.

Original (from the reading):

The costs of maintaining a solar energy system are very low.

Direct quote: The author states, "The costs of maintaining a solar energy system are very low."

Indirect quote: The author says that the costs of maintaining a solar energy system are very low.

Paraphrase: Solar energy maintenance costs are low.

Tip	Be careful not to simply copy text from the reading passage. Your score will be lowered if you copy.

Tip	When you refer to a reading passage, you can use *author* or *writer*. When you refer to a lecture, you can use words like *speaker, lecturer,* or *professor*. You can also use *man* or *woman* (depending on the speaker's gender).

These verbs are useful for citing.

Useful words

assert	describe	report
according to	explain	state
believe	note	say
claim	point out	suggest
confirm	propose	tell
contend	remark	think
deny	remind	warn

Practice

Rewrite the original statement as a direct quote, an indirect quote, and a paraphrase. Use as many different verbs as possible.

1. Original (from the reading): *Parents can inquire about what their children are doing in class.*

    Direct quote: _____

    Indirect quote: _____

    Paraphrase: _____

2. Original (from the lecture): *Many homeowners simply don't have the financial ability to install solar panels.*

    Direct quote: _____

    Indirect quote: _____

    Paraphrase: _____

3. Original (from the reading): *Aromatherapy has proven to be a popular form of treatment for both psychological and physical ailments.*

    Direct quote: _____

    Indirect quote: _____

    Paraphrase: _____

4. Original (from the lecture): *The only effect shown was that lemon oil appears to have a positive effect on mood.*

    Direct quote: _____

    Indirect quote: _____

    Paraphrase: _____

5. Original (from the reading): *Forest fires can have natural or human causes.*

   Direct quote: _____

   Indirect quote: _____

   Paraphrase: _____

6. Original (from the lecture): *For these reasons, a modern approach to forest fire management has developed, that recommends fighting only those fires caused by human activity or that threaten places where people live.*

   Direct quote: _____

   Indirect quote: _____

   Paraphrase: _____

7. Original (from the reading): *Industrial agriculture approaches food production in much the same way a factory approaches the production of manufactured goods.*

   Direct quote: _____

   Indirect quote: _____

   Paraphrase: _____

8. Original (from the lecture): *Crop rotation, in addition to maintaining soil health, also helps control pests by interrupting their breeding cycle.*

   Direct quote: _____

   Indirect quote: _____

   Paraphrase: _____

Independent Writing Task

Skill 1   The Main Idea–Your Opinion

In the Independent Writing Task you will be given a topic and asked your opinion on the topic. Your opinion will be the main idea of your essay. The main idea will determine *what* you write and *how* you will write.

Example

Question

In your opinion, what are the qualities of a good teacher? Use specific details and examples to support your answer.

Possible main ideas

1. A good teacher is a nice person.

Discussion: This idea is not complete. It tells only one quality of a good teacher, and that is a very vague one. What does it mean to be a "nice person"? This idea is not concrete or complete enough to serve as the basis for an essay.

2. A good teacher is one who is knowledgeable, creative, and kind.

Discussion: This is a complete idea that answers the question and can serve as the basis of a good essay. It mentions three qualities of a good teacher. The essay can be developed by discussing each of the three qualities.

3. Our schools do not have enough good teachers.

Discussion: This is a very clear opinion, however, it does not answer the question. The question asks about *qualities* of a good teacher. This main idea fails to mention qualities.

Practice

Read the following Independent Writing Task questions. Choose two statements that would be good main ideas and could be the basis of a good essay.

1. **It has recently been announced that a new shopping mall may be built in your neighborhood. Do you support or oppose this plan? Why? Use specific reasons and details to support your answer.**

   (A) Shopping malls make shopping convenient for everybody.
   (B) In my opinion, shopping malls are crowded and unpleasant places, so I never go to them.
   (C) I believe that a new shopping mall in my neighborhood is a great idea because it would bring jobs to the area and would make shopping more convenient.
   (D) I am opposed to a new shopping mall because it would bring traffic, noise, and crowds to my quiet neighborhood.

2. **Children get a better education at a small school rather than at a large one. Do you agree or disagree with this statement? Use specific reasons and examples to develop your essay.**

   (A) Large schools have several advantages over small schools, including more resources, more classes to choose from, and a greater variety of teachers.

(B) Depending on where you live, you might not be able to choose between a large school and a small school.

(C) At a small school, children get more attention to their individual educational, social, and emotional needs.

(D) I disagree that small schools are better because I went to a large school and I really enjoyed it.

3. **Which would you prefer: to work at a job that you did not enjoy but that paid a high salary, or to work at a job that you enjoyed very much but that paid only a modest salary? Use specific reasons and details to support your opinion.**

(A) We need money to pay for our basic needs as well as to buy some of the luxuries of life, and this is the major reason why we work.

(B) Spending every day at a job you do not like can have negative effects on your health, your family life, and your emotional well-being.

(C) If you work hard at your job, you can earn a lot of money and have a secure life.

(D) Some professions pay high salaries, while others do not.

4. **Many families have pets. Do you think it is important for a family to have pets? Why, or why not? Use specific reasons and examples to develop your essay.**

(A) A lot of people are allergic to dogs and cats, so they prefer pets such as turtles and fish.

(B) Pets can teach children some important things, such as a sense of responsibility and compassion.

(C) I think the most common reason people have pets is for companionship.

(D) It takes a lot of money and time to care for pets properly, and not all families are able to provide everything a pet needs.

Skill 2   Writing the Introduction

The introduction to an essay tells the reader what you plan to say. It is the most important part of your essay.

Example

Compare these two introductions.

Weak Introduction

> We have all had good teachers and bad teachers in our lives. In my opinion, a good teacher is one who is respected by her students.

Good Introduction

> It is not easy to be a good teacher. It takes a special person to do the job well. In my opinion, a good teacher is one who is knowledgeable, creative, and kind.

The weak introduction tells us only the writer's opinion, but gives us nothing to support that opinion. The good introduction outlines three specific points to explain the writer's opinion of what makes a good teacher: knowledgeable, creative, kind. These three specific points (general ideas) will form the body of the essay—one general idea for each paragraph.

Clearly identifying your ideas in a list such as this will help the reader follow your organization.

Main Idea: A good teacher is one who is knowledgeable, creative, and kind.

General Idea 1 (par. 1):   A good teacher is knowledgeable.

General Idea 2 (par. 2):   A good teacher is creative.

General Idea 3 (par. 3):   A good teacher is kind.

Practice

A. *Read the following introductions. Write the main idea of the essay and the general ideas of each paragraph.*

1. **Question**

It has recently been announced that a new shopping mall may be built in your neighborhood. Do you support or oppose this plan? Why? Use specific reasons and details to support your answer.

Introduction

My neighborhood is in a residential area far from our city's downtown. The people who live here have to travel far every day to get to work and to shop. I believe that a new shopping mall in my neighborhood is a great idea because it would bring jobs to the area and would make shopping more convenient.

Main Idea: _____

_____

General Idea 1:   _____

General Idea 2:   _____

2. **Question**

Children get a better education at a small school rather than at a large one. Do you agree or disagree with this statement? Use specific reasons and examples to develop your essay.

Introduction

Parents have to consider several things when choosing schools for their children. Location and cost are two factors, and size is also an important consideration. From my point of view, large schools have several advantages over small schools, including more resources, more classes to choose from, and a greater variety of teachers.

Main Idea: _____

_____

General Idea 1:   _____

General Idea 2:   _____

3. **Question**

Which would you prefer: to work at a job that you did not enjoy but that paid a high salary, or to work at a job that you enjoyed very much but that paid only a modest salary? Use specific reasons and details to support your opinion.

Introduction

If you work, you spend a large part of every day at your job. While it is important to earn money, of course, other things in life are important, too. Spending every day at a job you do not like can have negative effects on many aspects of your life, especially on your family relationships, your emotional well-being, and your physical health.

Main Idea: _____

_____

General Idea 1: _____

General Idea 2: _____

4. Question

Many families have pets. Do you think it is important for a family to have pets? Why, or why not? Use specific reasons and examples to develop your essay.

Introduction:

Families have pets for a variety of reasons, and many families are able to take good care of their pets. However, pets are not for everybody. It takes a lot of money and time to care for pets properly, and not all families are able to provide everything a pet needs.

Main Idea: _____

_____

General Idea 1: _____

General Idea 2: _____

B. *Now use your outlines to rewrite the introductions in your own words. Use a separate piece of paper, or use a computer.*

Skill 3   Writing a Paragraph

For the Independent Writing Task, you must use specific reasons and details to support your answer. Each paragraph in the body of your essay should have a general idea plus two or three supporting ideas. The supporting ideas can be examples. You need these details and examples to make the essay interesting and informative.

Here is an example outline and paragraph for General Idea 2.

Example

General Idea 2 (par. 2):   A good teacher is creative.

Supporting Detail 1:   She makes interesting lessons.

Supporting Detail 2:   She takes her students on field trips.

Supporting Detail 3:   She finds ways to help students who have difficulty.

A good teacher is certainly creative. She makes appealing lessons that get the students involved and help them understand the subject. She uses a variety of techniques in her lessons instead of teaching the same way all the time. In addition, she makes learning interesting by taking her students on field trips. In this way, she gives students the opportunity to learn outside of the classroom by visiting places and meeting people. A good teacher is also creative in finding ways to help students who have difficulty understanding the lesson. She can come up with different ways to explain things to them.

Practice

A. Read the question and the introduction below. Then read the paragraphs. Find the general idea and the supporting details of each paragraph. Write them on the lines.

Question

Children get a better education at a small school rather than at a large one. Do you agree or disagree with this statement? Use specific reasons and examples to develop your essay.

Paragraph 1 (Introduction)

Parents have to consider several things when choosing schools for their children. Location and cost are two factors, and size is also an important consideration. From my point of view, large schools have several advantages over small schools, including more resources, more classes to choose from, and a greater variety of teachers.

1. Paragraph 2

Children at a large school have access to a variety of resources that they might not have at a smaller school. A library at a large school has more materials than a library at a small school has. It has more books and magazines and probably has a variety of other materials such as CDs and DVDs, as well. In addition, the classrooms at a large school have more computers and more different kinds of software for the students to use. Furthermore, all these resources—books, magazines, computers, and software—are more likely to be kept up-to-date at a large school than at a small one.

General Idea: _____

Supporting Detail 1: _____

Supporting Detail 2: _____

Supporting Detail 3: _____

2. Paragraph 3

Children at a large school have more classes to choose from than they do at a small school. For example, instead of just general science or literature classes, they can choose from among different kinds of science or literature classes. They also probably have non-academic classes, such as art and music, available every day instead of just once a week or once a month, as at many smaller schools.

General Idea: _____

Supporting Detail 1: _____

Supporting Detail 2: _____

3. Paragraph 4

Children at a large school have the opportunity to learn from a greater variety of teachers. They can have a different teacher for each subject. This means they are taught by people who know their subjects well. It also means that they are exposed to different teaching styles, which enriches their learning experience. Additionally, they have many different adults around them to serve as role models. This is an important part of their education.

General Idea: _____

Supporting Detail 1: _____

Supporting Detail 2: _____

Supporting Detail 3: _____

B. *Now use your outlines to rewrite the paragraphs in your own words. Use a separate piece of paper, or use a computer.*

Skill 4   Stating Your Opinion

The introduction to your essay will tell the reader what you believe about the topic. There is no right answer. Your goal is to convince others that your opinion is correct.

Expressing Your Opinion

You can convince others that your opinion is correct by providing good supporting details and using certain phrases, verbs, adjectives, and adverbs to express your opinion.

Set Phrases	Verbs	Adjectives	Adverbs
From my point of view	agree	certain	absolutely
In my opinion	auxiliaries	confident	certainly
In my view	believe	convinced	conceivably
It is my opinion that	feel	persuaded	definitely
It seems to me that	guess	positive	doubtless
To me	hope	sure	maybe
To my mind	imagine		perhaps
To my way of thinking	suppose		possibly
Without a doubt	think		probably
			seemingly
			undoubtedly

Read the following sentences. Look for words and phrases from the list.

Certainly, a new shopping mall would greatly benefit our neighborhood.

It seems to me that the best teachers are the creative ones.

Earning money is probably the reason that most of us work.

To my way of thinking, every child should have a pet.

Practice 1

Give your opinion about these topics. Complete the sentences.

1. Small schools (provide/do not provide) children with the best possible education.
   It is my opinion that _____

2. Shopping malls (bring/do not bring) many benefits to the neighborhoods where they are located.
   In my view _____

3. Caring for pets (teaches/does not teach) children many important lessons about life.
   I suppose that _____

4. Having a lot of money (is/is not) more important than feeling happy in our daily life.
   I think that _____

5. Teachers who treat their students with kindness (are/are not) always appreciated.
   I am sure that _____

6. Shopping malls (have/do not have) a negative impact on the quality of life in the surrounding neighborhood.
   I am convinced that _____

7. A pet such as a dog or cat (is/is not) difficult for a young child to take care of.
   Perhaps _____

8. A high salary (can/cannot) compensate for an unpleasant work situation.
   Certainly, _____

Generalizing and Qualifying

Certain phrases can be used to make a general statement about how you feel about something. Others can be used to qualify your opinion, showing that what you state is not always true.

Generalizing	Qualifying
all in all	for all intents and purposes
as a rule	
basically	in a way
by and large	more or less
for the most part	so to speak
generally	to some extent
in general	up to a point
on the whole	

> **Tip** Notice that these phrases are separated from the rest of the sentence with commas when they appear at the beginning or in the middle.

Read the following sentences. Look for words and phrases from the list.

All in all, the best teachers are those who care about their students.

As a rule, large schools are better than small ones.

I feel that, to some extent, a good salary can make up for a boring job.

Smaller classes can be better for children up to a point.

Practice 2

Give your opinion about these topics. Complete the sentences to make a general statement or qualify your opinion.

1. Money does not buy happiness.

   As a rule, _____

2. Teachers at small schools have more time to pay attention to individual students.

   On the whole, _____

3. Pets are just an extra responsibility that modern families do not have time for.

   For the most part, _____

4. Shopping malls bring good jobs to a town or city.

   To some extent, _____

5. Strict teachers actually help their students more than kind teachers do.

   In a way, _____

Skill 5 Putting It All Together

You have seen how an essay is put together. Let's review the steps in the process.

1. Read the question carefully.

Question

In your opinion, what are the qualities of a good teacher? Use specific details and examples to support your answer.

2. Plan the introduction and paragraphs by making notes in an outline.

INTRODUCTION

Main Idea: *A good teacher is one who is knowledgeable, creative, and kind.*

GENERAL IDEA 1 (par. 1):   *A good teacher is knowledgeable.*
Supporting Detail 1:   *She has studied her subject in college.*
Supporting Detail 2:   *She continues to read about it.*
Supporting Detail 3:   *She knows her subject better than merely average teachers do.*

GENERAL IDEA 2 (par. 2):   *A good teacher is creative.*
Supporting Detail 1:   *She creates appealing lessons.*
Supporting Detail 2:   *She makes learning interesting by taking field trips.*
Supporting Detail 3:   *She finds ways to help students who have difficulty.*

GENERAL IDEA 3 (par. 3):   *A good teacher is kind.*
Supporting Detail 1:   *She cares about her students.*
Supporting Detail 2:   *She is patient with students who have difficulty.*
Supporting Detail 3:   *She is a friend as well as a teacher.*

3. Write the introduction.

It is not easy to be a good teacher. It takes a special person to do the job well. In my opinion, a good teacher is one who is knowledgeable, creative, and kind.

4. Write the body.

The most important quality of a good teacher, to my way of thinking, is that she is knowledgeable. In the first place, she has studied her subject in college, so she knows a lot about it. However it does not stop there. A good teacher keeps up-to-date in her field by continuing to read about it and study it throughout her career. A good teacher makes sure that she knows her subject better than teachers who are merely average.

A good teacher is certainly creative. She makes appealing lessons that get the students involved and help them understand the subject. She uses a variety of techniques in her lessons instead of teaching the same way all the time. In addition, she makes learning interesting by taking her students on field trips. In this way, she gives students the opportunity to learn outside of the classroom by visiting places and meeting people. A good teacher is also creative in finding ways to help students who have difficulty understanding the lesson. She can come up with different ways to explain things to them.

Finally, a good teacher is kind. She cares about her students, so she does her best to help them succeed. When students have difficulty understanding something, she doesn't get upset. Instead she works patiently to help them understand. Most of all, a good teacher is more than a teacher, she is a friend to her students. She is someone they can trust. Because of this, her students are not afraid to take risks or make mistakes. They are not afraid to learn.

A teacher who is knowledgeable, creative, and kind is well-equipped to help her students succeed in school. I wish we all could have (or be) good teachers.

5. You should add one more step before you finish. You should review your essay. Look over your work to make sure the essay is perfect. You'll learn more about review in the next section.

Practice

Create an outline for these topics and then write the essay. Use a separate piece of paper, or use a computer.

1. Your school has enough money to build either a new gym or a new library. Which should your school choose to build—a gym or a library? Use specific reasons and examples to support your recommendations.

2. Some people like to spend a vacation in one place, while others prefer to visit several different places in one vacation. Which type of vacation do you prefer? Use specific reasons and examples to support your choice.

3. Do you agree or disagree with the following statement? Modern children do not spend enough time outdoors. Use specific reasons and examples to support your opinion.

General Writing

Skill 1 Transition Words and Phrases

Transition words and phrases connect your ideas. These transitions help your reader follow your ideas from one sentence to the next or from one paragraph to the next. Transition words can show sequence, degree, comparison and contrast, and cause and effect. They can also be used to add additional information or to refer to something mentioned before.

Useful words and phrases

Time	Degree	Cause and Effect
after	above all	as a result
at the same time	first, firstly	because
before	in the first place	because of
meanwhile	in the second place	consequently
next	less important	due to
since	most important	for this reason
soon	principally	owing to
then	primarily	since
while	second, secondly	so
	third, thirdly	so that
	to a lesser degree	therefore
		thus

Look for words and phrases from the above list in these examples.

Example 1

From my point of view, a new shopping mall in my neighborhood would bring more problems than benefits. First, during the construction period there will be a lot of noise and dirt at the construction site. Meanwhile, we will have to endure heavy construction vehicles traveling through the neighborhood at all hours. After the mall is completed, people will come from all over to shop there. As a result, traffic in our neighborhood will increase.

Example 2

In my opinion, earning a high salary is very important. In the first place, we need to be able to pay for our basic necessities, such as food and clothing. At the same time, we all like to have luxuries such as nice vacations, more comfortable houses, and maybe even private school for our children. Above all, a high salary is a measure of respect. It reflects your status at your place of work and within your profession.

Useful words and phrases

Comparison	Contrast
also	although/even though
at the same time as	but
both	different from
in the same way	however
just as	in contrast to
like	nevertheless
likewise	on the other hand
similarly	unlike
similar to	yet

Look for words and phrases from the above list in this example.

Example 3

Large schools offer students a variety of resources that are often not available at small schools. Small schools, however, offer children a greater sense of security. Older students might do well in larger schools. Young children, on the other hand, need the feeling of safety that a small school offers. Both large schools and small schools can provide children with a good education, but small schools are the better choice for young children.

Useful words and phrases

Explanation	Adding More Information
for example	also
for instance	as well as
in other words	besides
like	furthermore
namely	in addition
such as	moreover
that is	what's more
to clarify	
to illustrate	

Look for words and phrases from the above list in this example.

Example 4

I enjoy spending my vacations traveling from place to place. I like seeing what different cities look like. It is also fun to meet all different kinds of people. In addition, I like visiting a lot of different museums, parks, and other tourist sites. In other words, I want to see as much as possible when I travel.

Practice

Read the following paragraphs. Choose the appropriate transition word or phrase from the box below each paragraph. Use a capital letter where needed.

Children these days definitely spend too much time indoors. (1)_____, they are in school all day. (2)_____ when they get home, they stay inside doing their homework or watching television. This is one reason why children often have health problems. If they spent more time outdoors, (3)_____, they would be much healthier. They would have the opportunity to get all kinds of physical exercise (4)_____ playing sports or riding bicycles.

in the first place	such as	then	on the other hand

Our school has a nice gym that is very large and in good condition. (5)_____ the gym, our library is in need of renovations. Many of the rooms could use a new coat of paint. (6)_____, a lot of things should be replaced. The elevators, (7)_____, are very old and often break down. (8)_____, I think we should spend money on fixing up the library.

unlike	for example	therefore	furthermore

From my point of view, it is a very good idea for families to have pets. Children usually enjoy taking care of pets. (9)_____ they are feeding the cat or walking the dog, they are learning some important lessons about responsibility. (10)_____, they develop a sense of compassion. (11)_____, pets provide children with a special kind of companionship. (12)_____ I think every family should have at least one pet.

moreover	while	at the same time	for these reasons

Skill 2 Synonyms

Using synonyms will provide variety in your essay. This variety will keep the reader interested and is an important element in paraphrasing. In addition, synonyms connect ideas across paragraphs without repeating the same word. This helps makes your writing more cohesive.

Read the paragraph below. Look for synonyms of *bad*.

bad: poor unpleasant awful terrible

   The gym at my school is very old and is in bad condition. It needs a lot of repairs. The roof leaks and the swimming pool has cracks. The locker rooms are unpleasant because everything in them is so old. The exercise room is in a very poor state. The floors and walls are awful and most of the equipment is broken. The basketball court is also in a terrible state of repair and should be entirely renovated.

Practice

Read each paragraph. Replace the second underlined word with a synonym from the box.

benefits   construct   draw   duties   easy   imaginative   sufficient

1. A good teacher is <u>creative</u>. He can develop interesting activities for his students because he is <u>creative</u>.

    creative   synonym: _____

2. The library we have now is <u>adequate</u> for our needs. It has <u>adequate</u> space for books and other materials.

    adequate   synonym: _____

3. A family pet gives children the opportunity to take on <u>responsibilities</u>. Children can be assigned daily <u>responsibilities</u> such as feeding the cat or walking the dog.

    responsibilities   synonym: _____

4. A shopping mall would make shopping much more <u>convenient</u> for everyone in my neighborhood. This would be good for the stores because people tend to spend more money when shopping is <u>convenient</u>.

    convenient   synonym: _____

5. Small schools have several <u>advantages</u> over large schools. One of the most important <u>advantages</u> is that children get more individual attention.

    advantages   synonym: _____

6.   I think it is an excellent idea to <u>build</u> a shopping mall in my neighborhood. If we <u>build</u> new stores, we will all have better places to shop.

build   synonym: _____

7.   It isn't always easy to <u>attract</u> good teachers to small schools. Larger schools tend to <u>attract</u> the better teachers.

attract   synonym: _____

Skill 3   Pronouns

Using pronouns to refer to nouns provides variety in your essay and helps the reader make connections. It is important to make sure that your pronouns agree in number and person and that they are the right part of speech.

Tip	Understanding pronoun reference is an important skill in reading as well as in your writing. The Reading section often includes questions about pronoun reference.

Pronouns

Subject:	I	you	he	she	it	we	they
		this	that	these	those		
Object:	me	you	him	her	it	us	them
		this	that	these	those		
Possessive adj.:	my	your	his	her	its	our	their
Possessive:	mine	yours	his	hers	its	ours	theirs

Practice

Find the noun that each underlined pronoun refers to.

I believe a new shopping mall would be welcome in <u>my</u> neighborhood. <u>It</u> would give people here a convenient place to shop. Right now, people in my neighborhood have to travel to the other side of town to do most of <u>their</u> shopping. A local shopping mall would make things much more convenient for all of <u>us</u>. For years, the mayor of our city has been talking about encouraging stores to locate in this part of town. So far, <u>she</u> has done nothing about this situation. <u>This</u> is something that has been very frustrating for my father and other older people. <u>He</u> would be very happy to have this problem solved by the construction of a new shopping mall.

Skill 4 Parallel Structures

Parallel structures are grammar structures that have the same pattern. For example, if you use two verbs in a sentence, they should be the same tense. Similarly, both verbs should be singular or both should be plural. The same is true for nouns.

Using parallel structures makes your writing easy to understand. It also provides variety. The readers will look for your ability to use parallel structures.

Examples

subjects

not parallel   <u>Working</u> and <u>play</u> are both important parts of a child's development.

In this example, the subjects are not parallel. The first is a gerund, and the second is a simple noun.

parallel   <u>Walking the dog</u> and <u>feeding the cat</u> are examples of tasks that most children can handle.

<u>Work</u> and <u>play</u> are both important parts of a child's development.

The subjects in both of the above examples are parallel. In the first example, they are both gerunds, while in the second example they are both simple nouns.

verbs

not parallel   We <u>walked</u> through the park and <u>were eating</u> ice cream cones.

New lockers <u>should be bought</u> and they <u>should repaint</u> the pool.

The verbs in these examples are not parallel. In the first example, the verbs are in different tenses—simple past and past continuous. In the second example, one verb is passive voice and the other is active voice.

parallel   We <u>walked</u> through the park and <u>ate</u> ice cream cones.

New lockers <u>should be bought</u> and the pool <u>should be repainted</u>.

The verbs in each of these examples are parallel because they follow the same form. In the first sentence, they are both in the simple past tense. In the second example, they are both passive voice.

other structures

parallel   Students at small schools <u>might get</u> more individual attention and <u>feel</u> more secure.

It is not necessary to repeat an auxiliary verb (such as *might*, *will*, or the verb *be* in a continuous tense) to keep verbs parallel within a clause.

not parallel   Shopping is <u>fun</u>, and I <u>enjoy</u> it.

This example is grammatically correct, but it is not parallel. It uses an adjective, *fun*, and a verb, *enjoy*, to describe shopping.

parallel   Shopping is <u>fun</u> and <u>enjoyable</u>.

This example is parallel because the words it uses to describe shopping are the same kind of word. They are both adjectives.

Practice
Change the second underlined word or phrase to make it parallel with the first.

1. When children take care of pets, they <u>can learn</u> to be responsible and <u>are having</u> fun at the same time.

2. <u>Working</u> all day at a dull job and then <u>to go</u> home tired and grumpy is not a good life.

3. A large school can make some children <u>feel uncomfortable</u>, and <u>it scares them</u>.

4. The teacher <u>graded</u> our papers every weekend, and <u>they were given back</u> to us on Monday.

5. I <u>was working</u> at an office during the day and <u>studied</u> for my college degree at night.

6. In my opinion, a shopping mall is a good place to shop because of its <u>variety</u> and <u>it is convenient</u>.

7. A dog needs to <u>be walked</u> every afternoon, and then <u>someone should feed it</u>.

8. <u>Creativity</u> as well as <u>being resourceful</u> are important qualities for a teacher to have.

Skill 5 Coherence
Coherence shows the relationship between sentences and between ideas. You can provide coherence to your essay by repeating words and rephrasing ideas.

Repeating
You can add rhythm to your essay by repeating some words and phrases. In the paragraph below, notice how the phrase *they provide children* is used several times and how it emphasizes the relationship among the three sentences.

Example
Parents choose smaller schools because they meet some of the most important needs of young children. *They provide children* with a warm, loving atmosphere. *They provide children* with many opportunities for individual attention. Most important of all, perhaps, *they provide children* with a strong sense of security.

 Tip The current example uses repetitions intentionally, not accidentally. Be careful not to overuse a word or phrase. Look at your writing in the final stage, and see if you need to rephrase instead.

Rephrasing
You can make your point stronger by rephrasing words and phrases. The reader then has another opportunity to understand your idea. You can rephrase a word with a synonym (see Skill 2). You can also rephrase a phrase or sentence by writing it in a different way.

The italicized words and phrases in the example paragraphs have a similar meaning.

Examples

People have pets because they make good *companions*. Dogs, for example, are very loyal *friends*.

Many people need a lot of *money* in order to feel secure. They want to know that they have enough *material wealth* to provide for all their needs and desires.

Some people are *addicted to shopping*. This can be a very serious problem in some cases. People who *cannot control their urge to buy things* often go into debt.

Practice

Choose the word, phrase, or sentence that best completes the paragraph. Use the italicized words as a guide.

1. Happiness means different things to different people. *For some people, it means having a lot of money and possessions. For others, it means developing their skills and talents as much as possible.* _____ Each one of us has to seek our own kind of happiness.

   (A) Some people are happiest when surrounded by loving friends and family.
   (B) Having loving friends and family makes some people quite happy.
   (C) For still others, it means being surrounded by loving friends and family.

2. It is very important for me to feel *satisfied* with my job. No salary, no matter how high, can make up for lack of _____, in my opinion.

   (A) career fulfillment
   (B) lifelong friends
   (C) retirement benefits

3. A good teacher is *knowledgeable* about his subject. Things change rapidly in the modern world, and new discoveries are always being made. A good teacher makes a point of _____ about the latest developments in his field.

   (A) teaching his students
   (B) staying informed
   (C) assigning interesting topics

4. As a rule, modern families are too busy to provide pets with the proper care and attention. *They are too busy to clean up after their pets. They are too busy to take them to the vet for regular check ups.* _____. For these reasons, I think it is not a good idea for most families to have pets.

   (A) Also, their responsibilities are too many to give them time to spend with pets.
   (B) Most of all, they are too busy to spend time with their pets.
   (C) In addition, no one has room in their schedule to spend time with a pet.

5. *Many people* enjoy going to shopping malls, and that is exactly the reason I don't like them. I always feel uncomfortable in (5)_____. I would much rather stay quietly at home.

(A) big buildings
(B) clothing stores
(C) large crowds

Skill 6 Sentence Types

You can vary your sentences by using a variety of sentence types. There are four types of sentences: simple, compound, complex, and compound-complex. Varying the types of sentences you use makes your writing more interesting.

Simple sentence

A simple sentence consists of one clause. That is, it has one subject and one verb.

Dogs make good pets.

subject verb

Compound sentence

A compound sentence consists of two or more simple sentences connected with a conjunction: *and, but, or.*

A mall will bring jobs to the neighborhood, and it will make shopping easier.

simple sentence 1   simple sentence 2

Complex sentence

A complex sentences consists of a simple sentence (independent clause) and one or more subordinate clauses (dependent clauses).

Because I have always studied at small schools, I know nothing about large schools.

subordinate clause   simple sentence

Compound-complex sentence

A compound-complex sentence consists of two or more simple sentences and one or more subordinate clauses.

Because I have always studied at small schools, I know nothing about large schools

subordinate clause   simple sentence 1

and I don't feel qualified to comment on them.

simple sentence 2

Practice

Read the following essay and label the sentences by their type.

Simple=S   Compound=C   Complex = Cx   Compound-Complex=C-Cx

---

1. _____   People often enjoy having pets around, but I do not think that every family
2. _____   should have them. Pets require a lot of time and attention.
   1
3. _____   Many families cannot give pets the care that they need.
   2
   3

4. _____   Pets demand a lot of time from their owners.
   4
5. _____   They need daily feeding.
   5
6. _____   Dogs need daily walking.
   6
7. _____   All pets need to be groomed frequently, and they need to be taken to a
            veterinarian regularly.   7
8. _____   Many families don't have time for these things.
   8

9. _____   Pets require a lot of attention.
   9
10. _____   Most pets do not like being alone.
   10
11. _____   If a pet is left by itself all day, it can become very depressed.
   11
12. _____   However, most people have to go to work or school, and they cannot be home
            during the day very often.   12
13. _____   This makes a sad life for a pet.
   13

Skill 7   Punctuation

You must be careful of your spelling and punctuation. In the Writing section, you will not have access to dictionaries or automatic spell checkers on the computer. Make sure you understand how each of the following is used.

➢ An **indent** of approximately a centimeter is made at the beginning of each paragraph.

➢ **Capital letters** are used at the beginning of each sentence and as the first letter for all proper nouns.

➢ A **period, question mark,** or **exclamation point** is always used at the end of a sentence.

➢ **Commas** are used in the middle of sentences in certain situations.

- In a list of three or more things

  Some small schools provide students with laptop computers, the latest software, and Internet access.

- To separate transition words from the rest of the sentence

  Additionally, a new gym would cost much more than a new library.

DIRECT TO TOEFL iBT™

– Between two independent clauses

I usually spend my vacation in one place, but I traveled to several different places on my last vacation.

– To separate a non-restrictive clause

My son, who is an exceptionally talented young man, has done very well at a small school.

– After a subordinate clause at the beginning of a sentence

After earning only a modest salary for several years, I realized that earning a decent amount of money is very important indeed.

Practice

Correct the punctuation errors in these sentencse. You can rewrite the sentences on a separate sheet of paper, or you can write on a computer.

1. there are many people who should not have pets. my neighbor for example is an irresponsible pet owner. he has three large dogs. he is gone all day and his dogs are left alone to bark loudly from morning until evening. this is sad for the dogs and unpleasant for all the neighbors. do you think it is a good idea for a person like this to have pets.

2. when I take a vacation I prefer to visit a city. in my opinion cities are fun and exciting places to visit. recently I spent a vacation in new york city which is a popular place for tourists. my days there were filled with fun activities such as shopping visiting museums and going to the theater. I was busy every day but I still did not see everything. if I get my wish I will visit there again sometime soon.

3. it seems to me that the best idea is to spend the money building a new library. the library we have now has many problems. the roof leaks many windows are broken and the heating system does not work well. because the library is such an uncomfortable place to be students do not like to use it. how much would it cost to build a new library. I do not know the answer to this question but I am sure the school administrators could find the money somewhere. it is very important for a school to have a good library.

4. earning a good salary is very important. if you are a professional you have a college education. you studied hard to get your degree and you probably paid a lot of money for your tuition. moreover you are expected to do professional-quality work at your job. for all these reasons you deserve to be paid well.

Skill 8 Revision

When you have finished your essay, take a few minutes to read it over. Ask yourself the questions in the following Review Chart.

Review Chart

	TASK
	Did I complete the task?
	Did I write enough words?
	Did I complete the task on time?
	FLOW
	Did I write a strong introduction?
	Did I write a main idea sentence for each paragraph?
	Did I write supporting details in each paragraph?
	VOCABULARY
	Did I use transition words?
	Did I use a variety of vocabulary?
	GRAMMAR
	Did I use parallel structures?
	Did I use a variety of sentence patterns?
	Did I use correct spelling and punctuation?

Let's compare the essay below with the Review Chart.

Question

In your opinion, what are the qualities of a good teacher? Use specific details and examples to support your answer.

Essay

It is not easy to be a good teacher. It takes a special person to do the job well. In my opinion, a good teacher is one who is knowledgeable, creative, and kind.

The most important quality of a good teacher, to my way of thinking, is that she is knowledgeable. In the first place, she has studied her subject in college, so she knows a lot about it. However, it does not stop there. A good teacher keeps up-to-date in her field by continuing to read about it and study it throughout her career. A good teacher makes sure that she knows her subject well, better than people generally do.

A good teacher is certainly creative. She makes appealing lessons that get the students involved and that help them understand the subject. She uses a variety of techniques in her lessons instead of teaching the same way all the time. In addition, she makes learning interesting by taking her students on field trips. In this way, she gives students the opportunity to learn outside of the classroom by visiting places and meeting people. A good teacher is also creative in finding ways to help students who have difficulty understanding the lesson. She can come up with different ways to explain things to them.

Finally, a good teacher is kind. She cares about her students, so she does her best to help them succeed. When students have difficulty understanding something, she does not get upset. Instead, she works patiently to help them do well. Most of all, a good teacher is more than a teacher, she is a friend to her students. She is someone they can trust. Because of this, her students are not afraid to take risks or make mistakes. They are not afraid to learn.

A teacher who is knowledgeable, creative, and kind is well-equipped to help her students succeed in school. I wish we all could have (or be) good teachers.

TASK

Review Chart

	TASK
	Did I complete the task?
	Did I write enough words?
	Did I complete the task on time?
	FLOW
	Did I write a strong introduction?
	Did I write a main idea sentence for each paragraph?
	Did I write supporting details in each paragraph?
	VOCABULARY
	Did I use transition words?
	Did I use a variety of vocabulary?
	GRAMMAR
	Did I use parallel structures?
	Did I use a variety of sentence patterns?
	Did I use correct spelling and punctuation?

Did I complete the task?

The question asks the writer for an opinion about the qualities of a good teacher. The introduction in the sample essay mentions three qualities of a good teacher: *knowledgeable, creative, kind*. The question also asks for details and examples. The second, third, and fourth paragraphs each explain one of the qualities mentioned in the introduction using details and examples.

Did I write enough words?

This passage is 322 words, well over the required minimum of 300 words.

Did I complete the task on time?

The task was completed in less than 30 minutes.

FLOW

Review Chart

	TASK
	Did I complete the task?
	Did I write enough words?
	Did I complete the task on time?
	FLOW
	Did I write a strong introduction?
	Did I write a main idea sentence for each paragraph?
	Did I write supporting details in each paragraph?
	VOCABULARY
	Did I use transition words?
	Did I use a variety of vocabulary?
	GRAMMAR
	Did I use parallel structures?
	Did I use a variety of sentence patterns?
	Did I use correct spelling and punctuation?

Did I write a strong introduction?

The last sentence of the first paragraph, *In my opinion, a good teacher is one who is knowledgeable, creative, and kind*, is the main idea of the essay. It states the writer's opinion, which is explained and supported in the body of the essay.

Did I write a main idea sentence for each paragraph?

The first sentence of each paragraph in the body of the essay (paragraphs 2, 3, and 4) is the main idea sentence.

Did I write supporting details in each paragraph?

Each main idea sentence is followed by details that support it.

VOCABULARY

Review Chart

	TASK
	Did I complete the task?
	Did I write enough words?
	Did I complete the task on time?
	FLOW
	Did I write a strong introduction?
	Did I write a main idea sentence for each paragraph?
	Did I write supporting details in each paragraph?
	VOCABULARY
	Did I use transition words?
	Did I use a variety of vocabulary?
	GRAMMAR
	Did I use parallel structures?
	Did I use a variety of sentence patterns?
	Did I use correct spelling and punctuation?

Did I use transition words?

This passage uses appropriate transition words, for example:

Paragraph 2:   *in the first place*—introduces the first idea

Paragraph 3:   *in addition*—adds information

　　　　　　　also—adds information

Paragraph 4:   *finally*—introduces a final idea

　　　　　　　most of all—shows degree

Did I use a variety of vocabulary?

This passage uses a variety of ways to state similar ideas, for example, synonyms *subject* and *field* in paragraph 2, *appealing* and *interesting* in paragraph 3, and *succeed* and *do well* in paragraph 4.

GRAMMAR

Review Chart

	TASK
	Did I complete the task?
	Did I write enough words?
	Did I complete the task on time?
	FLOW
	Did I write a strong introduction?
	Did I write a main idea sentence for each paragraph?
	Did I write supporting details in each paragraph?
	VOCABULARY
	Did I use transition words?
	Did I use a variety of vocabulary?
	GRAMMAR
	Did I use parallel structures?
	Did I use a variety of sentence patterns?
	Did I use correct spelling and punctuation?

Did I use parallel structures?

There are no sentences that are awkward because of lack of parallel structure.

Did I use a variety of sentence structures?

This passage uses a variety of sentence structures, for example:

Simple: *A good teacher is certainly creative.*

Complex: *When students have difficulty understanding something, she does not get upset.*

Compound-complex: *She makes appealing lessons that get the students involved and that help them understand the subject.*

Did I use correct spelling and punctuation?

This passage has no spelling or punctuation errors.

Practice

Complete each essay by answering the questions that follow.

Question 1

Which would you prefer: to work at a job that you did not enjoy, but that paid a high salary, or to work at a job that you enjoyed very much, but that paid only a modest salary? Use specific reasons and details to support your opinion.

Essay 1

If you work, you spend a large part of every day at your job. While it is important to earn money, of course, I feel that other things in life are important, too. Spending every day at a job you do not like can have negative effects on many aspects of your life, especially on your family relationships, your emotional well-being, and your physical health.

(1)_____ If you spent all day doing something you did not enjoy, you would not have the energy to be pleasant to your family when you got home in the evening. At best, you would choose to spend your evenings resting quietly alone. At worst, you would be in a bad mood and act grumpy around everyone. Either way, you would not enjoy a pleasant time with your family. Over time, your relationship with your family would deteriorate. No amount of money can make up for this.

Working every day at a job you do not like can have bad consequences for your emotional well-being. (2)_____ You might feel bored, angry, depressed, or all of these things, most of the time. It would be hard to relax and feel good in the evenings or on weekends after spending all day and all week at a job you did not like. Even a high salary would not be enough to make you feel happy.

(3)_____ If you felt unhappy most of the time, you probably would not have the energy to go to the gym, play a sport, or even take a walk. You would not get the physical exercise that you need. (4)_____, you would probably get sick frequently. Studies have shown a relationship between depression and the immune system. Depressed people get sick more often than people who are not depressed. So, you might earn a high salary, but you might also be too unhealthy to enjoy it.

---

1. Choose the best topic sentence for this paragraph.
    (A) Working every day at a job you do not like can have a bad effect on your family life.
    (B) If you do not enjoy your job, at least you should earn a good salary.
    (C) The best way to spend your time is doing something that you enjoy and can do well.

2. Choose the missing supporting detail.
    (A) If you did not enjoy your job, your family life might also become unhappy.
    (B) If you did not enjoy your job, your boss would notice and you might not get pay raises and promotions.
    (C) If you did not enjoy your job, you would be in a bad mood most of the time.

3. Choose the best topic sentence for this paragraph.
    (A) If you do not like your job, you might end up with poor physical health.
    (B) Working every day at a job you do not like can result in poor physical health.
    (C) Your health could suffer if you feel unhappy at work.

4. Choose the missing transition word.
    (A) Nevertheless
    (B) In addition
    (C) Next

Question 2

It has recently been announced that a new shopping mall may be built in your neighborhood. Do you support or oppose this plan? Why? Use specific reasons and details to support your answer.

Essay 2

Many people like to have shopping malls nearby. They make shopping convenient and they bring business to an area. I agree that these are good things.

(1) _____

We may not have a large mall in our neighborhood, but we do have some stores. We have several grocery stores, a hardware store, a drugstore, and even a small bookstore. These stores are not big, and they do not offer a huge variety of merchandise. (2) _____, they are enough to provide for our everyday needs. We do not have to leave the neighborhood to buy any basic necessities.

(3) _____. It is a quick trip to get to it by bus or by car. There is a large variety of stores there where you can buy just about anything you can think of. Since we can go to that mall so easily, I do not see any reason to build another one in our neighborhood.

Finally, but perhaps most important of all, I do not think there would be enough business here to make a mall worthwhile. My neighborhood is not crowded and the population is small. It is also not in a very convenient location. (4) _____ .
If a mall were built here, I think the store owners would find that they could not do enough business in this part of town.

A shopping mall would not bring any real benefits to my neighborhood and would probably not be successful here. These are the reasons why I am opposed to the plan.

---

1. Choose the best thesis statement.

   (A) However, I rarely go to shopping malls because all the malls in my city are located on the other side of town and I do not have any way to get to them.

   (B) On the other hand, shopping malls can bring many problems to an area, so both the advantages and disadvantages have to be considered.

   (C) Nevertheless, I am opposed to a shopping mall in my neighborhood because we already have stores here as well as a mall downtown, and I do not think there would be enough business here to make a mall worthwhile.

2. Choose the missing transition word.

   (A) However

   (B) In addition

   (C) As a result

3. Choose the best topic sentence for this paragraph.

   (A) When we need to buy things that are not available in our neighborhood, we can go to the shopping mall downtown.

   (B) The downtown shopping mall is one of the largest in our city and many people shop there.

   (C) There is a large shopping mall downtown that is one of the major tourist attractions in our city.

4. Choose the missing supporting detail.

   (A) Unfortunately, there are not any pretty parks or other nice places to take walks.

   (B) However, there are several attractive building sites that would be perfect for a mall.

   (C) It is far from all the other shopping areas in town, and I do not think many people would want to come over here to go shopping.

Question 3

Many families have pets. Do you think it is important for a family to have pets? Why, or why not? Use specific reasons and examples to develop your essay.

Essay 3

Many families have pets, and in my view this is a good thing. (1) _____. Owning a pet also provides children with the opportunity to develop a sense of responsibility and to learn some important life lessons, as well. I think every family should have at least one pet.

Certain kinds of pets make very good companions, and this is often the main reason families have them. Dogs, cats, birds, and other kinds of animals are fun for children to play with. Throwing a ball for a dog or teaching a bird to do tricks are pastimes that are both enjoyable and constructive. Having pets around can also give children a sense of security. A child who is afraid of the dark, (2) _____, can feel comforted by having the family dog sleep in the same room.

Children who care for pets learn to develop a sense of responsibility. Pets need to be fed one or more times a day. This has to be done even if you are busy, tired, or just do not feel like doing anything. In addition, pets need attention from their owners every day. Dogs need to be walked, and all pets need to be petted or played with. (3) _____. They need to be bathed or brushed frequently. Children quickly learn that if they do not take proper care of their pets, then the pets suffer.

(4) _____. They learn that all living creatures need proper care to grow and stay healthy. They learn about birth, and they learn how to cope with sadness when a beloved pet dies. Most of all, they learn that all of us, pets and people alike, want to have our needs met.

---

1. Choose the best general idea to complete the introduction.
   - (A) Dogs and cats are the most common pets to have.
   - (B) Pets make great companions for children.
   - (C) It can be quite expensive to own a pet.

2. Choose the missing transition word or phrase.
   - (A) therefore
   - (B) however
   - (C) for instance

3. Choose the missing supporting detail.
   - (A) In addition, pets like to be held and touched.
   - (B) Pets also have to be kept clean.
   - (C) Not all pets need a lot of exercise, however.

4. Choose the best topic sentence for this paragraph.
   - (A) Having pets around gives children the opportunity to learn some important things about life.
   - (B) Children are kept busy most of the time when they have pets to take care of.
   - (C) Pets are fun and interesting, and most children enjoy having them around.

Skills Practice

Integrated Writing Task

Read the passage. You have three minutes.

As people age, it is normal to experience occasional forgetfulness. Failing to remember where you put your keys or why you entered a room are common experiences. Forgetting names of acquaintances or public figures or not being able to call up a word that is on the tip of your tongue are other examples of ordinary age-related forgetfulness. These types of experiences are normal, do not seriously disrupt daily life, and are not an indication of more serious problems.

Aging people may also experience Mild Cognitive Impairment (MCI), a condition which is more serious then normal age-related forgetfulness. MCI prevents people from remembering things, such as appointments or names of family members. This slowdown in cognitive functioning can cause disruptions to daily routines, but people suffering from it can usually continue to lead independent lives. MCI may or may not develop into even more serious conditions, such as Alzheimer's disease or other forms of dementia.

During the aging process, the brain becomes less able to protect itself from processes such as inflammation and oxidation, which damage the brain tissues. In addition, Alzheimer's disease appears to be connected to the build-up in the brain of a substance called amyloid plaque. Plaque build-up leads to more inflammation and oxidation, and brain cells start to die off. Another thing that happens with age is that brain cells stop communicating with each other, and this also affects memory.

The good news is that there are a number of things people can do to prevent serious memory loss as they age. Getting enough sleep and exercise and managing stress are very important. So is eating a healthy diet. Eating fruits and vegetables high in antioxidants such as vitamins A, C, and E will protect brain cells from the oxidation process. Eating foods high in B vitamins, such as whole grains and green, leafy vegetables, also protects the brain.

 Listen to the lecture on a related topic.

Summarize the points made in the lecture, and explain how they strengthen the points made in the reading.

You have 20 minutes to respond. (Write on a separate piece of paper, or write on a computer.)

DIRECT TO TOEFL iBT™

Independent Writing Task

Write an essay of at least 300 words on the following topic:

Do you agree or disagree with the following statement?

Technology has made the world a better place to live.

Use specific reasons and examples to support your opinion.

You have 30 minutes to respond. (Write on a separate piece of paper, or write on a computer.)

Writing Samples

Sample responses to the Direct to TOEFL iBT™ Integrated and Independent Writing Tasks, with scores, can be seen at www.directtotoeflibt.com.

WRITING PRACTICE TEST

Integrated Writing Task

Read the passage. You have three minutes.

Concerns about the effect that violent television programs may have on behavior, particularly on children's behavior, have been around almost since the invention of television. Different types of research studies have been done in an attempt to answer the question: Does seeing violence on television lead to aggressive behavior?

In the early years of television, several studies were done on the immediate effects of watching violent television programs. In 1956, a study was done with a group of 24 children. Half of the children watched a *Woody Woodpecker* cartoon that contained violence, while the other half of the children watched a cartoon, *The Little Red Hen*, that contained no violence. Following the cartoon viewing, researchers observed the children as they played together. They noted that the children who had seen the violent cartoon had a much greater tendency to engage in violent behavior, such as hitting other children and breaking toys, than did the children who had seen the nonviolent cartoon.

In 1963, a study was done comparing the effects of watching real-life violence, violence on television, and violence in a cartoon. The study was done with 100 children who were divided into four groups. Three of the groups saw different versions of the same scene: a person shouting at and hitting a doll with a mallet. One group watched the scene live, another saw it on television, and the third saw it as a cartoon. The fourth group was not shown anything. Later, the children were observed as they responded to a frustrating situation. The children who had seen the live and television versions of the scene responded more aggressively to the situation than the children who had seen nothing.

These were some of the earlier studies that showed a relationship between violent programs and aggressive behavior.

 Listen to the lecture on a related topic.

Summarize the points made in the lecture, and explain how they strengthen the points made in the reading.

You have 20 minutes to respond. (Write on a separate piece of paper, or write on a computer.)

DIRECT TO TOEFL iBT™

Independent Writing Task

Write an essay of at least 300 words on the following topic:

Your city has enough money to build either a new history museum or a new park. Which should your city build?

Use specific reasons and examples to support your opinion.

You have 30 minutes to respond. (Write on a separate piece of paper, or write on a computer.)

READING

Read the following passages and answer the questions. You may take notes.

Passage 1

Male and Female Communication Styles

1   Differences in the ways men and women communicate is a subject that has been continually discussed by psychologists, anthropologists, linguists, and anyone who has had a relationship with someone of the opposite sex. Deborah Tannen, a linguistics professor at Georgetown University, has written a number of books about male/female communication differences; her books explore gender communication at home, at work, and in public discourse.

2   Tannen bases her theories on extensive research and observations of men and women in conversation. She believes that boys and girls begin learning different communication styles from an early age. She cites experiments in which researchers observed both men and women interacting with infants that were unfamiliar to them. When the subjects being observed believed the baby to be female, they cuddled it more. However, when they believed the baby to male, participants were more physically active with it and held it less. Tannen suggests that such research demonstrates how boys and girls are socialized differently from infancy. A brother and sister can grow up in the same household and yet learn very different ways of interacting and communicating with others. In fact, she asserts, conversation between men and women is actually intercultural communication.

3   Tannen talks about the different ways that men and women use conversation. She theorizes that conversation is used by women to establish connections and develop intimacy. Talking, particularly about troubles, forms the basis for friendship. Men, on the other hand, base their friendships on shared activities, such as fishing or playing sports, rather than on talking. Men use conversation to negotiate their status in a group and to preserve their independence.

4   It is not difficult to see how misunderstandings can occur. ■ (A) While a man may not want to discuss his problems, or even admit that he has any, because it puts him in a weaker position, a woman feels such conversation is necessary to maintain closeness. ■ (B) In a relationship, Tannen notes, a woman wants her partner to communicate anything that hurts him so she can stop doing it. However, if she asks the same of him, he may see complying with the request as putting him in a disadvantageous position in a relationship. ■ (C) In an insecure situation, the man is likely to resist requests while the woman is likely to be extra accommodating. ■ (D)

5   In a work environment, these stylistic differences manifest themselves in different ways. Women's communication style favors consensus building, but that can often emerge as a belief that everyone should be in agreement. During negotiations, a woman may look to balance her opinion with the concerns of others, while a male colleague simply goes for what he wants and expects others to do the same. Similarly, women are trained to feel that displaying excellence is lording it over others, while men grow up

knowing that promotions and raises are based on how others perceive your performance at work.

6   Tannen also sees these communication differences displayed at a macro level in public discourse. She labels this discourse "the argument culture" because so often people assume that the best way to discuss an idea is to debate it. Training in argument begins in high school and college classrooms; students are encouraged to debate topics, and teachers assume learning is taking place. However, often it is only a few students, frequently male, who participate in such discussions. The rest of the students, including the consensus-building girls, may feel uncomfortable and simply watch.

7   Tannen points to the increase in litigation in the United States to demonstrate how people tend to think that argument, rather than trying to work out differences in a non-conflictive way, is the only way to get things done. When women do not employ such discourse patterns, they are accused of lacking forcefulness or being too nice. Instead, they are encouraged to be ruthless and tough. While Tannen does not oppose spirited debate, she sees our culture reflexively turning to argument as the automatic response to every situation. Tannen also perceives this ethic of controversy as pervading the media. Journalists and pundits see it as their job to describe controversies and to frame everything in polarizing terms. She views criticisms of politicians as being ritualized so much that public attacks are de rigeur for public figures. Journalists feel that if they do not take a hard line, they are not doing their jobs.

8   Tannen's ability to take her theories from home to work to public discourse demonstrates how pervasive gendered communication is and how important it is to be aware of it.

---

1. **The author discusses the way adults interact with babies in paragraph 2 in order to make the point that**
   (A) boys and girls are born with different personality traits
   (B) both men and women enjoy communicating with babies
   (C) babies learn about male and female differences at an early age
   (D) babies need to interact with adults to learn how to communicate

2. **The word status in paragraph 3 is closest in meaning to**
   (A) membership
   (B) friendship
   (C) entrance
   (D) position

3. Look at the four squares (■) in paragraph 4 that indicate where the following sentence could be added.

   Conversely, when a woman asks for help or advice, a man may see her as weak or lacking self-confidence.

   Where would the sentence best fit?

4. The word accommodating in paragraph 4 is closest in meaning to
   (A) helpful
   (B) pleasant
   (C) demanding
   (D) comfortable

5. According to paragraph 5, which of the following is true about gender differences in communication at work?
   (A) Women favor certain people's ideas over others.
   (B) Men are generally more demanding than women.
   (C) Men assume that women will state their wants directly.
   (D) Women are not expected to express opinions in negotiations.

6. The phrase lording it over in paragraph 5 is closest in meaning to
   (A) acting superior to
   (B) asking for help from
   (C) showing strength to
   (D) sharing with

7. According to paragraph 6, all of the following are true about debate-based discussions EXCEPT:
   (A) They are usually dominated by a few people.
   (B) They are common in high schools and classrooms.
   (C) Girls tend to participate despite feeling uncomfortable.
   (D) Teachers often see them as a learning tool.

8. According to paragraph 7, how does Tannen feel about debate as a form of communication?
   (A) It is almost always a bad idea.
   (B) People in the United States rely on it too much.
   (C) It is the only way to get things done.
   (D) Women should be encouraged to use it.

9. The word polarizing in paragraph 7 is closest in meaning to

(A) editorializing

(B) opposing

(C) critical

(D) political

10. The word they in paragraph 7 refers to

(A) politicians

(B) public attacks

(C) public figures

(D) journalists

11. Which of the following sentences best expresses the information in the highlighted sentence in paragraph 8?

(A) The fact that Tannen's theories can be applied to different kinds of situations shows how relevant they are.

(B) If people were more aware of Tannen's abilities, they would understand the importance of her theories.

(C) Tannen's ability to communicate her theories at home, at work, and in public has made many people aware of her important work.

(D) The theories that Tannen has developed about discourse at home, at work, and in public have made many people aware of gendered communication.

12. Complete the chart below to summarize information about male and female communication styles. Match each phrase with the communication style it describes. This question is worth 3 points.

Male	•
	•
	•
Female	•
	•

Answer Choices

(A) Cuddling is the major way to communicate with babies.

(B) Conversation is an essential part of friendship.

(C) Friendships are strengthened by doing things together.

(D) Discussing troubles is a sign of weakness.

(E) Finding ways to agree is important.

(F) Debating issues feels comfortable and natural.

(G) Communication is ritualized.

Passage 2

Women's Suffrage

1 The women's suffrage movement in the United States was not, as many may believe, a twentieth-century phenomenon. There are records dating back as far as colonial America that show attempts by women to have a voice in government. Those efforts continued in an ebb-and-flow fashion for more than two hundred years until American women were finally given the right to vote in 1920, and the struggle for equal rights for women continues today.

2 While some men in colonial America supported women's rights—most notably, founding father Thomas Paine—the commonly held view of women in the 1600s was that they were "inferior beings" who were not allowed to own anything, whether property, their earnings, or even their own children. Legally speaking, women were no different from slaves, criminals, and the insane.

3 In 1648, a woman named Margaret Brent attempted to change this. Brent was the first female landowner in the colonies as well as the first female lawyer. She was also the first woman to try to obtain the right to vote. Her business successes led her to become executor of Maryland Governor Leonard Calvert's estate. It was after Calvert's death in January 1648 that Brent demanded two votes in the state assembly: one for herself as a landowner, and one representing Calvert because she held his power of attorney. Brent's request was denied by reason of her gender. There is no further evidence to suggest that Brent continued her crusade. It would be another 200 years before the next documented women's suffrage movement took place at the Seneca Falls Convention.

4 The idea for the convention held in Seneca Falls, New York was sparked by events at the World Anti-Slavery Convention in London in 1840. ■ **(A)** It was there that Lucretia Mott and Elizabeth Cady Stanton met as American delegates to the convention. ■ **(B)** Eight years later, they met again in Seneca Falls, where Stanton lived. ■ **(C)** They discussed the recent passage of the New York Married Women's Property Act, legislation that granted married women the right to own their own property. ■ **(D)** Believing the law did not go far enough, the women decided to hold a convention "to discuss the social, civil, and religious condition and rights of women". Drawing ideas from the Declaration of Independence, Stanton wrote a Declaration of Sentiments, the document that became the foundation of the convention.

5 The convention drew about 300 people, including 40 men, one of whom was Frederick Douglass, a former slave who had become a powerful and outspoken newspaper editor. During the five-day convention, all the Declaration's resolutions were passed except for the one calling for women's suffrage. Days later, newspapers such as the New York Herald derided the meeting, but in so doing, they printed the Declaration in its entirety. Stanton was ecstatic over the publicity, asserting that it would start women thinking and men, too. She felt that the first step toward progress had been taken.

6 While their cause was largely sidelined during the Civil War (1861–1865), it regained momentum in the late 1860s, when feminists found themselves split over the proposed

15th Amendment to the Constitution, which gave voting rights to black men. Susan B. Anthony and Elizabeth Cady Stanton were incensed that the amendment did not address women's right to vote. Others supported the amendment, theorizing that once black men were enfranchised, women's enfranchisement would soon follow.

7   In 1872, two years after black men were given the right to vote, Susan B. Anthony was arrested for casting a ballot in a presidential election. During her trial, Anthony made one of the most legendary speeches of her time. "[I] simply exercised my citizen's rights, guaranteed . . . by the National Constitution. The preamble of the Federal Constitution says . . . we, the people; not we, the white male citizens; nor yet we, the male citizens; but we, the whole people . . . women as well as men." Despite her eloquent defense, Anthony was fined $100, which she refused to pay.

8   In 1890, the National American Woman Suffrage Association (NAWSA), headed by Anthony, began seeing the results of their state voting rights campaigns. Colorado became the first state to grant women the right to vote, and over the next decade a dozen other states followed suit. By 1919, Congress had enough votes to pass a federal law giving all women the right to vote. The 19th Amendment to the U.S. Constitution, ratified August 18, 1920, states that "The right of citizens of the United States to vote shall not be denied or abridged by the United States or by any State on account of sex". That same year NAWSA became the League of Women Voters, a nonpartisan organization still in existence today.

1. **Why does the author discuss Margaret Brent in paragraph 3?**
   (A) To give an example of an early attempt to gain voting rights for women
   (B) To describe how Maryland's political system operated in the 1600s
   (C) To illustrate how voting was carried out in colonial America
   (D) To explain the events leading to the Seneca Falls convention

2. **According to paragraph 3, what is one reason Margaret Brent believed she should have the right to vote in the state assembly?**
   (A) She was a lawyer.
   (B) She owned property.
   (C) She had a successful business.
   (D) She was a friend of the governor.

3. **The word crusade in paragraph 3 is closest in meaning to**
   (A) position
   (B) interest
   (C) career
   (D) fight

4. Look at the four squares (■) in paragraph 4 that indicate where the following sentence could be added.

   However, they were denied seats and barred from addressing the assembly because they were women.

   Where would the sentence best fit?

5. According to the information in paragraph 5, what can be inferred about the Seneca Falls convention?

   (A) Men had not been invited to attend.
   (B) Douglass was the only journalist present.
   (C) Issues in addition to voting rights were discussed.
   (D) The Declaration of Sentiments was rewritten by the attendees.

6. The word derided in paragraph 5 is closest in meaning to

   (A) reported
   (B) attended
   (C) ridiculed
   (D) protested

7. According to paragraph 5, how did Stanton feel about the newspaper articles covering the Seneca Falls convention?

   (A) Cautious because she was not sure how men would react
   (B) Angry because they expressed disagreement with her goals
   (C) Happy because they brought public attention to her cause
   (D) Sad because she thought few people would read them

8. According to paragraph 6, what were Anthony and Stanton angry about?

   (A) Attention was taken away from the women's movement during the war.
   (B) Black men were being given the right to vote but women were not.
   (C) Feminists could not agree about the enfranchisement of black men.
   (D) A new amendment to the constitution had been proposed.

9. The word legendary in paragraph 7 is closest in meaning to

   (A) well-written
   (B) daring
   (C) lengthy
   (D) famous

10. According to paragraph 7, why was Susan B. Anthony given a $100 fine?

    (A) She voted before women had voting rights.

    (B) She refused to pay money that she owed.

    (C) She made a long speech that angered the judge.

    (D) She threatened the president of the United States.

11. According to paragraph 8, all of the following are true EXCEPT:

    (A) NAWSA focused efforts on women's suffrage in individual states.

    (B) Between 1890 and 1900, women gained the right to vote in 12 states.

    (C) Women were granted the right to vote in the United States by a constitutional amendment.

    (D) By 1890, Susan B. Anthony was no longer participating in the women's movement.

12. The word abridged in paragraph 8 is closest in meaning to

    (A) limited

    (B) granted

    (C) removed

    (D) controlled

13. An introductory sentence for a brief summary of the passage is given below. Complete the summary by choosing THREE answers that best represent the main ideas in the passage. This question is worth 2 points.

Women in the United States fought for the right to vote for a long time.

-

-

-

Answer Choices

(A) Margaret Brent was an unusual figure in colonial America because she was a female landowner and lawyer.

(B) Elizabeth Cady Stanton and Lucretia Mott met while working in the anti-slavery movement and worked together to draw attention to the cause of women's rights.

(C) The New York Married Women's Property Act, granting women property ownership rights, was passed in 1848, eight years after Elizabeth Cady Stanton and Lucretia Mott first met.

(D) Less attention was focused on the women's rights movement during the Civil War, but there was renewed interest following the war, particularly when black men were given the right to vote.

(E) NAWSA worked to get individual states to grant women the right to vote until women throughout the country were granted voting rights by the 19th Amendment to the U.S. Constitution.

(F) NAWSA, as the League of Women Voters, is still a prominent political organization for women voters today.

Passage 3

The Dance of the Honeybee

1 Body language can be as simple as a raised eyebrow or more laden with meaning than the spoken word—and it is not limited to humans. From lizards doing push-ups to squirrels twitching their tails, creatures throughout the animal kingdom have fine-tuned the art of information exchange. One of the most remarkable and elaborate forms of communication is the waggle dance of the honeybee. This insect version of the hokey pokey not only communicates that a first-rate food supply is at hand, it also details how far away and in what direction the food is located, using the sun as a reference point.

2 Honeybees live in colonies of about 50,000 to 60,000 bees. Each hive has a single queen, a few hundred male drones, and many thousands of sterile female workers. The queen and drones have a straightforward job description: Reproduce. The workers do everything else—feed the queen, drones, and developing larvae; clean and ventilate the hive; build the wax combs to house the queen's eggs and to store food; collect nectar and pollen and process them into honey; and protect the home territory from invaders. Keeping the hive running efficiently and the residents healthy is a monumental job, not unlike running a small city. A well-organized system with a clear-cut division of labor and reliable lines of communication is a must.

3 When a honeybee scout spies an interesting patch of flowering vegetation, such as a field of sweet clover, she first samples it, sucking out nectar with her tongue and packing bits of pollen into tiny pouches on her hind legs. Then she heads home to tell her sisters. She will need their help carrying her loot back to the hive.

4 Inside the hive, a vertical comb doubles as a dance floor. If the clover is nearby— within a hundred yards or so—the scout delivers a quick, nonspecific message. She gyrates in a tight circle in a jig dubbed the "round dance" that tells her sisters food is close by. The dance prompts them to go out and forage, but they will use their own senses of smell and sight to find the food.

5 The waggle dance comes into play when the food source is farther away. The scout struts along the comb in a straight line waggling her abdomen, shaking her tail, and beating her wings to make buzzing noises. She stops and loops in a semicircle back to the starting point, waggles down the same path, and then circles back again in the opposite direction, outlining a wide figure eight in the process. Her sisters watch and decipher: the length of her straight line tells them the distance to the clover, and her orientation on the comb tells them the direction relative to the sun. A downward path means the clover lies directly away from the sun, straight up means it is directly toward the sun, and all other directions specify the angle between the hive and the sun; for example, a horizontal path on the comb means it is at a 90° angle to the sun.

6 People had long been aware of the waggle dance but not its meaning—not until some 60 years ago when an Austrian zoologist named Karl von Frisch proposed that the dance was a coded message to lead hive mates to food. In 1973, he won a Nobel Prize for his work. His theory met with widespread acceptance from the start, although a few

naysayers doubted the existence of such a complicated process in insects and believed individual bees simply followed the scout toward the food, and used their own senses of sight and smell to find it once they got close. A study in 2005 confirmed von Frisch's theory, with scientists putting tracking devices on bees and then following them as they made a direct path from the hive to the vicinity of the food. From that point, the bees searched around until they located the food on their own.

7   Today, most scientists agree that worker bees use the distance and direction information in their dances to locate food, but they generally agree that smell also plays an important role. While the scout dances, she flings pollen into the air, and waggle watchers get a good whiff of the scent of flowers. It may help them recognize the scout's distant clover field, or it may simply stimulate their appetite. Although they probably observe the whole dance, they do not all follow the dancer's directions. Some forego the long trek to the clover field and simply head to their favorite flower garden instead.

1. **The author mentions lizards and squirrels in paragraph 1 in order to make the point that**
   - (A) lizards and squirrels are as interesting as honeybees
   - (B) the use of body language is common among animals
   - (C) lizards and squirrels do not communicate with dances
   - (D) honeybees are better communicators than other animals

2. **According to the information in paragraph 2, what can be inferred about a honeybee colony?**
   - (A) There might be more than one queen in a colony.
   - (B) Drones help to clean and ventilate the hive.
   - (C) Female worker bees do not reproduce.
   - (D) The queen is always fed first.

3. **The word monumental in paragraph 2 is closest in meaning to**
   - (A) common
   - (B) routine
   - (C) hazardous
   - (D) huge

4. **According to paragraph 3, what is the first thing a honeybee does when she finds food?**
   - (A) She tastes some.
   - (B) She hides bits of it.
   - (C) She does a special dance.
   - (D) She takes it back to the hive.

5. The word loot in paragraph 3 is closest in meaning to

(A) information

(B) companions

(C) treasure

(D) flowers

6. According to paragraph 4, when a honeybee finds food close to the hive, what information does her dance convey?

(A) The distance the bees will have to fly

(B) The type of food that is available

(C) The exact location of the food

(D) The fact that food is near

7. The word forage in paragraph 4 is closest in meaning to

(A) dance

(B) follow

(C) hunt

(D) fly

8. According to paragraph 5, which part of the dance describes the route the bees will have to follow to find food?

(A) The shaking of the abdomen

(B) The direction of the dance

(C) The type of buzzing noise

(D) The length of the dance

9. The word decipher in paragraph 5 is closest in meaning to

(A) read

(B) count

(C) measure

(D) imitate

10. Which of the following sentences best expresses the information in the highlighted sentence in paragraph 6?

(A) Those who accepted von Frisch's theory tried to prove it by following honeybees as they went out to scout for food.

(B) Although many accepted von Frisch's theory, others said that honeybees simply followed a scout and used sight and smell to find their food.

(C) A few people doubted von Frisch's theory, but they thought it would be too complicated a process to show that he was wrong.

(D) Many people accepted von Frisch's theory at first, but as he tried to explain the complicated process used by bees, some began to doubt him.

11. **The highlighted word they in paragraph 7 refers to**

    (A) scientists
    (B) flowers
    (C) dances
    (D) bees

12. **According to paragraph 7, all of the following are true about the honeybee dance EXCEPT:**

    (A) Bees generally watch the entire dance.
    (B) Pollen is thrown around during the dance.
    (C) Watching the dance probably makes the bees hungry.
    (D) Bees always follow the instructions of the dance.

13. **An introductory sentence for a brief summary of the passage is given below. Complete the summary by choosing THREE answers that best represent the main ideas in the passage. This question is worth 2 points.**

    Honeybees use elaborate dances to communicate the location of food.

    -
    -
    -

Answer Choices

(A) A honeybee colony is quite large and consists of a queen, some male drones, and many female worker bees.

(B) According to the clearly defined division of labor in a honeybee colony, the worker bees are responsible for all the work of maintaining the colony, especially finding food.

(C) After a worker bee finds a source of food, she uses a dance to describe to the other bees the location of the food relative to the position of the sun.

(D) The honeybee dance involves waggling the abdomen, shaking the tail, and making a buzzing sound by beating the wings.

(E) An Austrian zoologist won a Nobel Prize for his work on honeybee dances and communication.

(F) Scientists have confirmed that honeybees use information from their dances to locate food, and also believe that the sense of smell plays an important role.

LISTENING

Listen to the following lectures and conversations and answer the questions. You may take notes.

Lecture 1

1. **What is this lecture mainly about?**

   (A) The ability of babies to see color

   (B) Ways to improve babies' vision

   (C) Vision problems among babies

   (D) How the eye perceives color

2. **What types of patterns are attractive to newborn babies?**

   (A) Patterns with strongly contrasting colors

   (B) Patterns with various shades of gray

   (C) Patterns with only a few colors

   (D) Patterns with many lines

3. **What does the professor imply about toy companies?**

   (A) Their products help the development of babies' vision.

   (B) They should make more colorful toys for babies.

   (C) They take advantage of parents' anxieties.

   (D) The patterns on their toys are too bright.

4. **Listen again to part of the lecture. Then answer the question.**

   What does the professor mean when she says:

   (A) She does not want the students to make any mistakes in their answers.

   (B) She is going to correct some wrong information that she gave earlier.

   (C) She believes it is wrong for parents to be overly concerned about vision.

   (D) She does not want the students to misunderstand her opinion of concerned parents.

5. **Which part of the eye helps us perceive color?**

   (A) The outer layer of tissue

   (B) The cones in the retina

   (C) The visual cortex

   (D) The lining

6. **Based on information in the lecture, indicate at what age a baby can perceive the colors listed below. For each color, put a check in the correct column. This question is worth 2 points.**

	0–1 month	2–3 months	4–5 months
Black and white			
Red and green			
Pastel shades			
Shades of gray: 5% contrast			
Shades of gray: less than 5% contrast			

Lecture 2

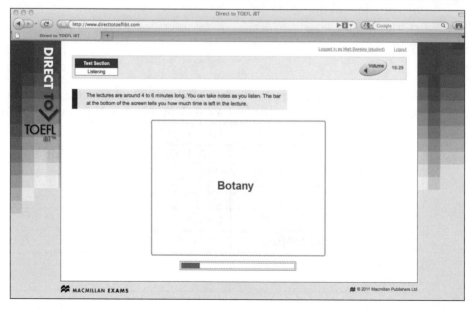

7. **What is this lecture mainly about?**
   (A) The lifecycle of deciduous trees
   (B) What happens to leaves in the fall
   (C) The different types of pigments in leaves
   (D) How deciduous and evergreen trees differ

8. **Listen again to part of the lecture. Then answer the question.**

   What does the professor mean when he says:
   (A) He wants to know who is interested in the topic.
   (B) He wants to know which students did the homework.
   (C) He wants to know whose turn it is to give a presentation.
   (D) He wants to know who can explain why leaves change color.

9. **Which color pigments are present in leaves during the growing season?**
   (A) green only
   (B) green, yellow, and orange
   (C) red only
   (D) red and purple

10. **Which weather condition can result in brilliant autumn foliage?**
    (A) A rainy spring
    (B) A late spring
    (C) A dry summer
    (D) A wet summer

11. **According to the lecturer, indicate which of the features of leaves listed below contribute to the changing of leaf colors in the fall. For each feature, put a check in the YES or NO column. This question is worth 2 points.**

	YES	NO
Chlorophyll levels		
Protective coating		
Sugars		
Watery sap		
Thin tissues		

12. **Listen again to part of the lecture. Then answer the question.**

    What does the professor mean when he says:
    (A) To call the students' attention to the information
    (B) To tell the students about something they will have to buy
    (C) To remind the students to ask for help if they do not understand
    (D) To announce that he is about to pass out some materials to the students

Lecture 3

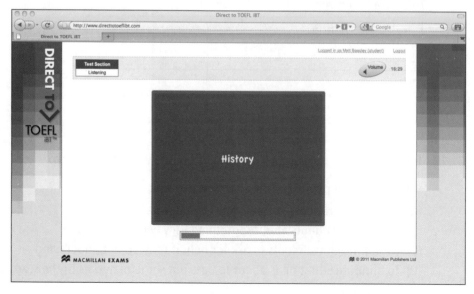

13. **What is this lecture mainly about?**

   (A) An English doctor's contribution to epidemiology
   (B) The problem of water contamination in London
   (C) Cholera epidemics in the nineteenth century
   (D) The historical development of anesthetics

14. **Listen again to part of the lecture. Then answer the question.**

   What does the professor mean when she says:

   (A) She wants students to remember this piece of information.
   (B) She plans to call on a student to comment on her point.
   (C) She is mentioning a point previously discussed.
   (D) She is introducing a new topic.

15. **Why does the professor mention the cholera outbreak among miners?**

   (A) To explain how Snow got his medical training in England
   (B) To describe some of the early treatments for cholera
   (C) To illustrate how primitive medical practice was at the time
   (D) To show an early inspiration for Snow's thinking

16. **What is the professor's opinion of the theory of miasma?**

   (A) It is a ridiculous idea.
   (B) It is important to understand.
   (C) It is an idea that is spreading.
   (D) It does not deserve attention.

17. **Why did Snow make a map of a London neighborhood?**

   (A) To show where the Broad Street pump was located
   (B) To prove his theory about the cause of cholera
   (C) To discover a local source for clean water
   (D) To help doctors find cholera victims

18. **What happened after the Broad Street pump handle was removed?**

   (A) Snow was asked to test other sources of water.
   (B) Residents protested the removal of the handle.
   (C) The local cholera death rate went down.
   (D) Snow's ideas gained wide acceptance.

Lecture 4

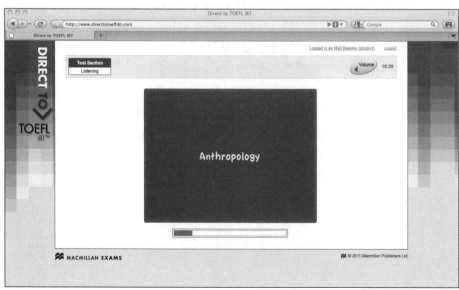

19. **What is this lecture mainly about?**

    (A) The history of the Navajo people

    (B) An overview of Navajo culture

    (C) The Navajo tradition of weaving

    (D) Spanish influence on Navajo culture

20. **Where do the Navajo live?**

    (A) northern Mexico

    (B) western Canada

    (C) northern United States

    (D) southwestern United States

21. **Why does the professor mention the Pueblo people?**

    (A) To explain the origin of Navajo weaving

    (B) To illustrate the effects of Spanish occupation

    (C) To describe the region prior to the Navajo arrival

    (D) To show the Navajo's relationship with their neighbors

22. **Which group originally introduced sheep to the Navajo?**

    (A) The Pueblo

    (B) The Spanish

    (C) The Mexicans

    (D) The U.S. government

23. **Based on information given in the lecture, indicate which of the following characteristics of weaving belong to which period. For each characteristic, put a check in the correct column. This question is worth 3 points.**

	Classic/Late Classic	Transitional	Rug
natural colors			
chemical dyes			
designs based on stripes			
designs influenced by traders			
designs including crosses and rectangles			

24. **Listen again to part of the lecture, then answer the question.**

    What does the professor mean when he says:

    (A) He is trying to remember a word.

    (B) He is asking the students for information.

    (C) He is reminding students about something they read.

    (D) He is telling the students to make a note of something.

DIRECT TO TOEFL iBT™

Conversation 1

DIRECT TO TOEFL iBT™

25. **What does the student need help with?**

    (A) Developing lesson plans for student teaching
    (B) Applying for a teaching job
    (C) Choosing a new student teaching site
    (D) Completing student teaching requirements

26. **What level is the student teaching now?**

    (A) Preschool
    (B) Elementary school
    (C) Middle school
    (D) High school

27. **Indicate which of the items below need to be included in the student teaching portfolio. For each item, put a check in the YES or NO column. This question is worth 2 points.**

	YES	NO
Observation forms		
Sample lesson plans		
Book reviews		
Teacher evaluation		
Journals		

28. **Listen again to part of the conversation. Then answer the question.**

    What does the professor mean when she says:

    (A) She does not want the student to misunderstand.
    (B) She is correcting a mistake the student just made.
    (C) She gave the student some incorrect information.
    (D) She wants to prevent any future errors.

29. **How does the student feel about the student teaching experience?**

    (A) It was too easy.
    (B) It was too much work.
    (C) It was hard but worth it.
    (D) It was a waste of time.

Conversation 2

30. **What does the student want to do?**
    (A) Register for her biology class
    (B) Get a class booklist for biology
    (C) Sell some used biology books
    (D) Buy things she needs for class

31. **Listen again to part of the conversation. Then answer the question.**

    What does the clerk mean when he says:
    (A) The book is not on a high shelf.
    (B) There are more copies of the book available.
    (C) The book is not especially expensive.
    (D) Some classes require more books.

32. **When does the biology class start?**
    (A) This afternoon
    (B) Tomorrow
    (C) In two days
    (D) Next week

33. **What does the clerk give the student?**
    (A) A lab manual
    (B) A used textbook
    (C) A pad of drawing paper
    (D) A list of art supplies

34. **What will the student do next?**
    (A) Look at the bulletin board
    (B) Buy a used lab manual
    (C) Go to art class
    (D) Go online

SPEAKING

Question 1

Question 2

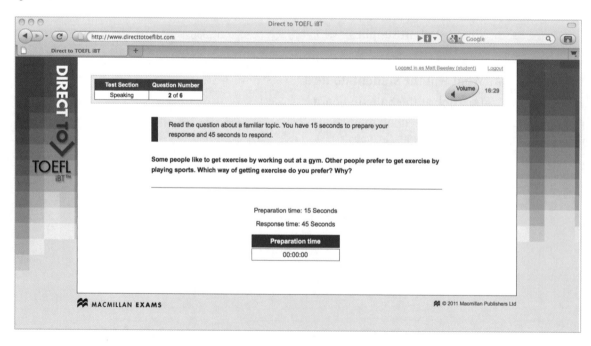

Question 3

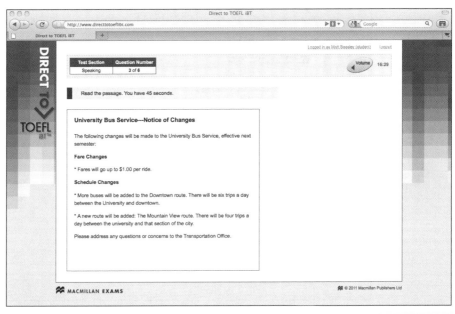

Read the passage. You have 45 seconds.

University Bus Service---Notice of Changes

The following changes will be made to the University Bus Service, effective next semester:

Fare Changes

* Fares will go up to $1.00 per ride.

Schedule Changes

* More buses will be added to the Downtown route. There will be six trips a day between the University and downtown.

* A new route will be added: The Mountain View route. There will be four trips a day between the university and that section of the city.

Please address any questions or concerns to the Transportation Office.

Listen to the speaker.

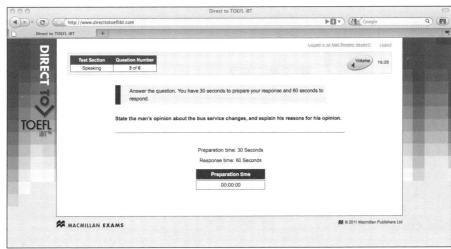

Answer the question. You have 30 seconds to prepare your response and 60 seconds to respond.

State the man's opinion about the bus service changes, and explain his reasons for his opinion.

Preparation time: 30 Seconds
Response time: 60 Seconds

Preparation time
00:00:00

Question 4

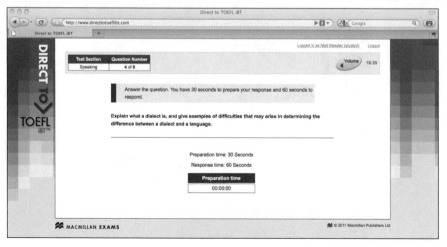

Question 5

Question 6

WRITING

Integrated Writing Task

Read the passage. You have three minutes.

Ethanol fuel, made from various types of plants, has been touted as the answer to our country's dependency on foreign oil and all the accompanying economic and environmental problems. Most cars currently on the road can run on a mix of 90% gasoline and 10% ethanol, and indeed this type of mix is sold in many places. Ethanol can be produced from sugarcane, potatoes, corn, and other plant material, but corn is the most popular material being used in the country.

Using corn-based ethanol as automobile fuel is not the answer to our oil-dependency problems that many would have us believe. In the first place, it is not particularly efficient. Considering the resources it takes to grow the corn, as well as to turn the corn into ethanol, the energy result is negative. It takes about 130,000 BTUs to make one gallon of ethanol, which in turn only produces about 75,000 BTUs to move your car. It also costs almost twice as much money to produce a gallon of ethanol as it does a gallon of gasoline. Then there is the environmental damage caused by the production of corn. Soil erosion and depletion of groundwater sources for irrigation are serious problems.

To say that converting to ethanol would solve our dependency on foreign oil is a false dream. It would take well over 97% of the land in the United States to grow enough corn to produce fuel for all the cars currently being driven in this country. In addition, land that is used to grow corn for ethanol is land that is not being used to grow food. Clearly, ethanol fuel is not the answer to our transportation problems.

 Listen to the lecture on a related topic.

Summarize the points made in the lecture, and explain how they challenge the points made in the reading.

You have 20 minutes to respond. (Write on a separate piece of paper, or write on a computer.)

Independent Writing Task

Write an essay of at least 300 words on the following topic:

Do you agree or disagree with the following statement?

Life in the city is much better than life in the countryside.

Use specific reasons and examples to support your answer.

You have 30 minutes to respond. (Write on a separate piece of paper, or write on a computer.)

DIRECT TO TOEFL iBT™